ART AT AUCTION 1982–83

ART AT AUCTION
The year at Sotheby's 1982–83

Two hundred and forty-ninth season

SOTHEBY PUBLICATIONS

© Sotheby Parke Bernet & Co. 1983

First published for Sotheby Publications by
Philip Wilson Publishers Ltd,
Russell Chambers, Covent Garden, London WC2E 8AA
and
Sotheby Publications,
Biblio Distribution Centre,
81 Adams Drive, Totowa, New Jersey 07512

ISBN 0 85667 180 0
ISSN 0084–6783

Editor: Tim Ayers
Assistant (London): Elizabeth Treip
Assistant (New York): Elizabeth White

Cover photograph by Norman Brand, art directed by Theo Hodges

Printed in England by Jolly & Barber Ltd, Rugby
and bound by W. S. Cowell Ltd, Ipswich

Note
Prices given throughout this book include the buyer's
premium, as applicable in the saleroom concerned. These
prices are shown in the currency in which they were realized.
The sterling and dollar equivalent figures for prices this
season, shown in brackets, are for guidance only and are
based on the rounded rates of exchange on 1 June 1983.
These rates for each pound sterling are as follows: Australian
dollars, 1.81; United States dollars, 1.60; Hong Kong dollars,
11.30; French francs, 12.08; Swiss francs, 3.35; Dutch guilders,
4.53; Italian lire, 2,385; South African rand, 1.72.

Sotheby's galleries at Bond Street and Bloomfield Place are
indicated by the designation 'London', and those at York
Avenue by the designation 'New York'.

Frontispiece
A bronze bust of Henry II of France by Germain Pilon, *circa* 1570, height of bust $27\frac{1}{8}$ in (69cm)
Monte Carlo FF 1,110,000 (£91,887 : $147,019). 13.II.83
From the collection of the Comte Antoine de Dreux-Brézé

Contents

CLAUDE MONET
Nymphéas
Stamped with signature, *circa* 1897–98, 51in by 59¾in (129.5cm by 151.8cm)
New York $2,640,000 (£1,650,000). 18.V.83

Opposite
JOHN RUSKIN
Amboise
Watercolour over pencil with scratching out, 1841, $17\frac{1}{4}$in by $11\frac{1}{4}$in (43.8cm by 28.5cm)
London £19,800($31,680). 30.III.83

Forty years later Ruskin commented on his youthful emulation of Turner, 'representing the castle as about seven hundred feet above the river (it is perhaps eighty or ninety) with sunset light on it, in imitation of Turner; and the moon rising behind it in imitation of Turner; and some steps and balustrades (which are not there) going down to the river, in imitation of Turner; with the fretwork of St Hubert's Chapel done very carefully in my own way, – I thought perhaps a little better than Turner.'

Preface

John Marion and Julian Thompson

The 1982–83 season has been a spectacular and memorable one as the art market emerged from the recession of 1982. The highlights were the record-breaking auction of Impressionist and modern paintings in New York, including works from the Havemeyer Collection, and the dispersal of the contents of Hever Castle in London (Figs 1–2). Other important individual lots have also achieved record prices in their respective fields. Still more significant has been the general improvement of prices at the medium and lower levels. In short, confidence and stability have returned.

In both major salerooms, the season has seen a consolidation of Sotheby's facilities. In New York this was the first year in a new North American headquarters, the specially designed galleries on Seventy-second Street and York Avenue. The flexibility of the space makes it possible to exhibit on three floors and to hold two or three auctions simultaneously. Meanwhile, in London, the opening of a gallery in the old Steinway Hall allows us to hold five sales at the same time in the Bond Street complex.

However, the true story of Sotheby's past season lies in the saleroom successes, reflected in the pages of this book. Auction history was made in an electrifying evening sale in New York, on 18 May, when ten Impressionist and modern paintings each exceeded a million dollars. This sale included sixteen works collected by Mr and Mrs H. O. Havemeyer, the great benefactors of the Metropolitan Museum of Art: Degas's pastel *L'attente* sold for $3,740,000, an auction record for an Impressionist work (Fig. 1). The whole sale totalled $37.2 million, more than any recorded art auction to date.

Sotheby's in New York has continued to reaffirm its traditional leadership in the field of American painting and Americana. *The Norther*, a bronze by Frederic Remington, chronicler of the American West, established an auction record for American sculpture ($715,000) and *Classic landscape*, a Precisionist work by Charles Sheeler, from the Edsel and Eleanor Ford House of Detroit, established a new record for a twentieth-century American painting ($1,870,000). The continuing demand for the finest American furniture was demonstrated by the sale of a Chippendale 'hairy-paw-foot' chair made for General John Cadwalader of Philadelphia, which fetched $275,000, the highest price ever paid for a chair. A Chippendale desk made by the Goddard–Townsend school sold for $687,500, an auction record for any piece of American furniture.

Fig. 1
The auction of Degas's *L'attente*, which fetched $3,740,000 (£2,337,500); John Marion taking the sale of Impressionist and modern paintings at York Avenue on 18 May 1983.

Fig. 2
The sale of the Negroli armour from Hever Castle, which made £1,925,000 ($3,080,000); Julian Thompson taking the auction of the Hever arms and armour in the main Bond Street saleroom on 5 May 1983.

Fig. 3
JOHN WEBBER, RA
Portrait of Captain James Cook
Signed and dated *1782*, 45½in by 36in (115.5cm by 91.5cm)
Melbourne Aus$506,000 (£279,558: $447,293). 23.III.83
From the collection of the Corporation of the Hull Trinity House

The April jewellery sale was another notable success, realizing more than $7 million, the highest total of any jewellery sale in the world last year. A sale of English furniture and works of art, held to coincide with the festivities celebrating the bicentenary of the Treaty of Paris, 'Britain Salutes New York', brought nearly $4 million. Turning to individual lots, an Egyptian granite statue of Merneptah, Royal Scribe and Charioteer to Rameses II, achieved a new auction record for an Egyptian antiquity ($341,000); a *sancai* glazed pottery jar fetched a world record for Tang pottery ($484,000), and more than thirty new auction records were set for individual artists.

In London, the magnificent arms and armour from the collection of the Lord Astor at Hever Castle turned the Bond Street galleries briefly into a repository for some of the finest examples of the Gothic and Renaissance armourer's craft: a Mannerist suit of armour made for Henry of Valois, King Henry II of France (1547–59), and decorated by Giovanni Paolo Negroli fetched nearly £2 million (Fig. 2).

Among other remarkable works of art sold in London were the long-lost cabinet made for Louis XVI's study at Versailles, identified by Sotheby's expert Jonathan Bourne, which became the most expensive piece of furniture ever sold at auction (£990,000); a Persian Polonaise carpet, which became the most expensive carpet (£231,000); Richard Dadd's masterpiece *Contradiction: Oberon and Titania*, painted while the artist was confined in Bethlem mental hospital (£550,000); a rediscovered ewer and basin made for an eighteenth-century Recorder of the City of Bristol, among the finest pieces of English Rococo silver (£176,000); and a hitherto unknown full-score working draft of Stravinsky's revolutionary *Le sacre du printemps* (£330,000).

In Europe, Sotheby Mak van Waay celebrated fifty years of auctions in their present building and in March achieved the highest price to be paid at auction in Holland, for Salomon van Ruysdael's *Winter in Utrecht* (DFl 1,020,800). Important lots in the Monte Carlo spring sales included a fine sketch for Fragonard's celebrated *Le verrou*, a Japanese lacquer commode by Bernard van Risenburgh II and a bronze bust of Henry II of France by Germain Pilon.

Further afield, a new office directed by Robert Bleakley was opened in Sydney, Australia, and their first sale took place at the Regent Hotel, Melbourne, in March. The most important lot was a portrait of Captain Cook by John Webber (Fig. 3), who travelled with Cook to the South Seas and survived the massacre on Hawaii in which the explorer was killed.

The buoyancy of sales this season has owed much to the impact of American buying on the international market. Among the important lots sold in London, both the Negroli armour from Hever and the French royal cabinet went to American private collectors. The results are most encouraging for the future. Quality is still the overriding factor, but we can now look forward to a more generous overall supply of works of art. Sellers have returned in force and buyers are now pursuing their collecting interests as vigorously as ever.

As this book was going to press, it was announced that Mr Alfred Taubman had been given clearance by the Secretary of State for Trade and Industry to proceed with his bid for Sotheby's. His acquisition of the company has the support of Sotheby's staff throughout the world and resolves in the best possible way the long takeover battle of the past year. We look forward to an exciting future under his chairmanship.

The American Art Association 1883–93: the first decade of Sotheby's forerunner in America

Thomas E. Norton

New York City enjoyed the atmosphere of a boom town in the late nineteenth century, with its mixture of old wealth, new money, increased trade and an exploding population. In May 1883, the 'Great Suspension Bridge' linking New York and Brooklyn was inaugurated with ceremony: it was the longest span in the world at the time. The Metropolitan Opera House opened in October with a gala performance of Gounod's *Faust*. Buildings were going up all over town, and European – especially French – paintings were selling briskly at Goupil's, Knoedler's and other dealers' establishments. In the midst of all this activity, a new organization, christened the 'American Art Association', opened for business on Madison Square, on East Twenty-third Street, just south of the park formed by the intersection of Broadway with Fifth Avenue.

A century ago, Madison Square was the centre of an unusually mixed neighbourhood, even for New York (Fig. 1). Grand hotels, elegant mansions, sober 'brownstones', stores and commercial establishments of every type existed side by side. The old railway terminal on Twenty-sixth Street had been renamed Madison Square Garden and converted into an entertainment centre by P. T. Barnum. The National Academy in its Venetian palazzo stood on Twenty-third Street, as did the Eden Musée, celebrated for its waxworks. Delmonico's restaurant and the Hoffman House, renowned for Bouguereau's *Satyr and nymphs* over the bar, were favourite watering holes.

It seems appropriate then that this neighbourhood should have been the birthplace of a commercial organization founded 'for the encouragement and promotion of American art'. The fledgling firm, the American Art Association, was destined to become the country's leading auctioneer and exhibitor of fine art and antiques within a decade, by astutely combining high ideals with a keen business sense.

The three co-founders were not strangers to the ways of the city's burgeoning art business. First of the trio, and the one with the capital, was James Fountain Sutton, a wealthy enthusiast of modern paintings and Oriental ceramics, who was the son-in-law of department-store magnate, R. H. Macy. Sutton's prior venture in the art trade had not been a success and the old firm was dissolved in 1882. His two new partners were R. Austin Robertson, who shared Sutton's love of Chinese artefacts, and Thomas E. Kirby, an ambitious and imaginative young auctioneer (Fig. 2). Space was rented in the Kurtz Photographic Building, at 6 East Twenty-third Street, and the new partnership was in business, with the premises known as the 'American Art Gallery'.

Fig. 1
ALESSANDRO GUACCIMANNI
Rainy afternoon, Madison Square
1892, 14in by 20in (35.5cm by 50.8cm)
Reproduced courtesy of the New-York Historical Society

This painting well conveys the atmosphere of Madison Square
in the early days of the American Art Association.

Fig. 2
A photograph of Thomas E. Kirby, aged seventy-five, one of
the three founders of the American Art Association

Business was slow, however, until a major exhibition of paintings by the respected American artist George Inness (1825–94) opened to the public in 1884 (Fig. 3). The *New York Tribune* hailed 'the broad range of the artist's powers illustrated in the remarkable exhibition', and noted that 'the catalogue contains an unusual amount of reading matter', which was a prophetic statement in view of the many informative catalogues that would appear in the coming years.

More space was leased, and in the catalogue of a show by contemporary artists, chosen to open the refurbished premises, Sutton, Robertson and Kirby expressed the desire 'to prepare a hospitable center where American Art can at last, after long waiting, be sure of a welcome . . . No cost has been spared.' Considering what had been done for them, the owners hoped that the artists would, in turn, 'lend a cordial and generous concurrence . . . and take full advantage of this, the first opportunity they have ever had, to place their pictures as they are painted, before the picture-loving and picture-buying public.' Despite the eloquent invitation to this new perpetual salon, the press was less than ecstatic about the works on display. One artist was singled out by the *Tribune* as having been inspired by Manet, 'the painter-in-chief of ugliness'. Public response was favourable, however, and the American Art Galleries soon became a fixture of the city's cultural life.

Then, in 1885, when George I. Seney, a prominent Brooklyn financier, was forced by creditors to sell his extensive collection of modern paintings, the American Art Association was asked to handle the auction. Kirby realized that this was a golden opportunity and convinced his less-than-enthusiastic partners that they should expand the business, while maintaining the firm's respectable and fashionable image. This could be accomplished, he argued, by upholding the high standard of the Association's exhibitions and catalogues and by 'managing' the auction as an important artistic, cultural and social event, far removed from the questionable and often shoddy practices of most auctioneers in the city at that time.

Accordingly, in mid-March 1885, a lavish catalogue was published and the pictures – 285 of them by Barbizon and academic European painters, plus a few Americans – tastefully displayed. When a critic for the *New York Post* questioned the authenticity and quality of several works in the sale, Kirby filed suit for libel and the resulting publicity made the pre-sale exhibition an enormous popular success. Both the trade and the Association's following of wealthy *amateurs* rose to the occasion: on the evenings of 31 March, and 1 and 2 April, police had to restrain the crowds outside Chickering Hall so that the ticket-holders could be seated for the auction. The grand total for the Seney pictures exceeded $400,000 and Jules Breton's *Evening in the hamlet*, reviled as 'a pathetic minor work' by the *Post*, made $18,200, the highest price of the sale and the talk of the town for a long time to come. The way the sale had been handled by Kirby and his colleagues was widely acclaimed and, however reluctantly the role of auctioneer was undertaken at first, the Association's successful debut in this field changed the destiny of the firm – and the way public sales would be conducted in the future.

Soon other auctions were held: in the autumn of 1885, the George Whitney Collection of paintings; in 1886, the Mary Jane Morgan sale of 2,628 lots of pictures, porcelain and other items from her house on Madison Square. In 1887, the dispersal

Fig. 3
GEORGE INNESS
Winter morning, Montclair
1882, 30in by 45in (76.2cm by 114.3cm)
Reproduced courtesy of the Montclair Art Museum, Montclair, New Jersey

This is one of fifty-seven works by Inness exhibited at the American Art Gallery in 1884.

of the contents of A. T. Stewart's fabulous marble mansion on Fifth Avenue and Thirty-fourth Street broke every record (Fig. 4). One of the nineteenth century's most celebrated paintings, Rosa Bonheur's *Horse fair*, was acquired by Cornelius Vanderbilt, who immediately presented it to the Metropolitan Museum of Art for exhibition in its new building in Central Park.

Major loan exhibitions, usually with admission fees, continued to be held by the Association (Fig. 5). In the spring of 1886, at James Sutton's invitation, the French dealer Paul Durand-Ruel presented 'Works in Oil and Pastel by the Impressionists of Paris', the first Impressionist exhibition ever held in the United States. The public reaction was such that Durand-Ruel soon opened a branch gallery in New York. America's long-standing love affair with Impressionism began on Twenty-third Street.

Collectors of more conservative taste were heartened when the American Art Association, in a stunning coup, acquired Millet's *Angelus*, perhaps his most famous picture, and exhibited it in New York. It was shown 'at the northern end of the top-most gallery, against a drapery of dark crimson plush fit for the setting of a throne'. In 1890, the *Angelus* was repatriated and given to the Louvre, but during its stay in

Fig. 4
CHILDE HASSAM
The Stewart Mansion, New York
Circa 1891, 18¼in by 22⅛in (46.4cm by 56.2cm)
Reproduced courtesy of the Santa Barbara Museum of Art (Gift of Sterling Morton for the Preston
Morton Collection)

This impressive building on Fifth Avenue and Thirty-fourth Street housed the collection of
A. T. Stewart, which was auctioned by the American Art Association in 1887.

New York, it was seen by thousands of people. Influential shows of Barye bronzes, Rodin sculpture and, in 1929, American furniture (the famous 'Girl Scout Exhibition') continued to generate good will and business for the American Art Association.

In 1892, R. Austin Robertson died, and Sutton soon retired from the firm. In 1922, Thomas Kirby oversaw the company's departure from Twenty-third Street and its move uptown to Madison Avenue and Fifty-seventh Street, after which he too retired. Hiram Parke and Otto Bernet, who had worked closely with Kirby, remained as the Association's managers until 1937, when they left to form their own auction gallery. Twenty-seven years later, in 1964, Parke-Bernet Galleries merged with Sotheby & Co. to form Sotheby Parke Bernet.

Fig. 5
GEORGES SEURAT
Sunday afternoon on the island of La Grande Jatte
1884–86, 81 in by 120⅜ in (205.8cm by 304.8cm)
Reproduced courtesy of the Art Institute of Chicago (Helen Birch Bartlett Memorial Collection)

One of Seurat's best-known works, *La Grande Jatte* was exhibited at the American Art Gallery in 1886.

Throughout this hundred-year history, generations of leading American families – Morgans, Havemeyers, Rockefellers, Vanderbilts, Chryslers, Fords – have entrusted their collections to the American Art Association, to Parke-Bernet Galleries and to Sotheby Parke Bernet. A Monet acquired by Henry O. Havemeyer at the American Art Association in 1900, for example, was sold by another generation of the family at Sotheby Parke Bernet in 1983.

Over the course of a century there have been many ups and downs, but traditions and practices established during the American Art Association's first decade on Madison Square continue to be honoured. Beautifully printed catalogues of entire collections or specialized sales are still published with a view to informing potential bidders. Pre-sale exhibitions continue to be carefully mounted in luxurious galleries, and direct participation by private collectors in the auction process is encouraged today, as it was in 1885. This approach, geared to an affluent constituency of self-reliant entrepreneurs, was considered radical in the 1880s, but has come to be adopted by the auction world internationally. These are the enduring contributions of the American Art Association, and the continuing tradition of Sotheby Parke Bernet in America.

Paintings and drawings

NERI DI BICCI
Virgin and Child enthroned with St James and St Andrew
On panel, signed, inscribed and dated $A \cdot D \cdot MCCCCLXIII$, $65\frac{3}{8}$in by $67\frac{1}{2}$in (166cm by 171.5cm)
Florence L 302,400,000 (£126,792:$202,867). 14.XII.82

The inscription reads: *QUESTA · TAVOLA · AFACTO · FARE · BASTIANO · DANDREA · DEBECCI · DACERTALDO · A · D · MCCCCLXIII*. The painting is mentioned in Neri di Bicci's *Ricordanze*, which reveal that it was commissioned by Otto Nicholini for his foreman, Bastiano da Certaldo. The *Ricordanze* describe the altarpiece in great detail and give the name of the artisan who prepared the panel, Luca Manucci. Work commenced on 4 March 1463 and the altarpiece was delivered on 22 July of the same year to the church of S. Spirito, Florence.

NICCOLO DI SEGNA
Virgin and Child
On panel, 27in by 17$\frac{7}{8}$in (68.5cm by 45.5cm)
London £71,500 ($114,400). 6.VII.83
From the collection of Captain P. J. B. Drury-Lowe of Locko Park, Derbyshire

BERNARDO BELLOTTO
S. Maria dei Miracoli with part of S. Maria Nova, Venice
Circa 1740, 16¼in by 26in (41.2cm by 66cm)
New York $198,000 (£123,750). 9.VI.83

GIOVANNI BATTISTA TIEPOLO
Mars and Venus
16⅛in by 28⅜in (41cm by 72cm)
Monte Carlo FF1,776,000(£147,020:$235,232). 26.VI.83

This is the *modello* for a ceiling in the Palazzo Pisani-Moretta, Venice.

JUSEPE DE RIBERA called LO SPAGNOLETTO
The Martyrdom of St Bartholomew
Signed and dated *1634*, 40½in by 44⅛in (103cm by 112cm)
London £660,000($1,056,000). 6.VII.83
From the collection of Colonel Cranstoun of that Ilk, MC

BARTOLOME ESTEBAN MURILLO
The Mystic Marriage of St Catherine
28in by 20½in (71.1cm by 52cm)
New York $209,000(£130,625). 20.I.83
From the collection of the late the Hon. Irving M. Scott

D. Angulo Iniguez and Jonathan Brown suggest that this is a sketch for the central portion
of Murillo's last major commission, the St Catherine altarpiece in the abbey church of the
Capuchins, Cadiz. The altarpiece was largely executed by Murillo's pupil Francisco
de Meneses Osorio, and the sketch may have served to guide him in his master's absence.

JEAN-HONORE FRAGONARD
Le verrou
On panel, 10¼in by 12¾in (26cm by 32.5cm)
Monte Carlo FF 2,775,000 (£229,719:$367,550). 14.II.83

This is a sketch for the large picture, now in the Louvre, commissioned by the Marquis de Veri.

JOACHIM ANTONISZ. WTEWAEL
Mars and Venus surprised by the gods
On copper, signed, 8in by $6\frac{1}{8}$in (20.3cm by 15.5cm)
London £253,000 ($404,800). 6.VII.83

JAN PROVOST
The Nativity
On panel, *circa* 1510, 20¼in by 15in (51.3cm by 38.1cm)
New York $154,000(£96,250). 20.I.83

GERARD DOU
An astronomer by candlelight
On panel, signed, 12⅝in by 8⅜in (32cm by 21.2cm)
London £121,000($193,600). 6.VII.83
From the collection of the Lord Astor of Hever

SALOMON VAN RUYSDAEL
Winter in Utrecht
On panel, signed with monogram and dated *165 (8 ?)*, 29¾in by 42⅛in (75.5cm by 107cm)
Amsterdam DFl 1,020,800 (£225,342:$360,547). 14.III.83

JAN VAN GOYEN
River scene
On panel, signed with monogram and dated *1655*, 18½in by 24⅜in (47cm by 62cm)
Amsterdam DFl 649,600 (£143,400:$229,440). 14.III.83

SALOMON VAN RUYSDAEL
Winter scene outside a town
On panel, signed with monogram and dated *1653*, 22in by 31½in (56cm by 80cm)
London £242,000 ($387,200). 6.VII.83

FRANS POST
A plantation in Brazil
On panel, signed and dated *1665*, 14in by 16⅛in (35.5cm by 41cm)
London £132,000 ($211,200). 9.III.83

PIETER BRUEGHEL THE YOUNGER
Peasants returning from the fair
On panel, signed, $16\frac{3}{8}$in by $22\frac{7}{8}$in (41.5cm by 58cm)
London £148,500 ($237,600). 17.XI.82
From the collection of the late Madame Marie Coulon

PIETER BRUEGHEL THE YOUNGER
The wedding procession
On panel, signed and dated *1627*, 29½in by 47½in (74.9cm by 120.7cm)
New York $231,000 (£144,375). 20.I.83

CORRADO GIAQUINTO
A kneeling Dominican
Black and white chalk on pink-washed paper,
15¾in by 10⅜in (40cm by 26.3cm)
London £5,720 ($9,152). 15.VI.83

GIOVANNI BATTISTA PIAZZETTA
Head of the guardian angel
Black chalk heightened with white on blue paper,
15¾in by 11⅞in (39.9cm by 30.1cm)
London £22,000 ($35,200). 18.XI.82

NICOLAES BERCHEM
Peasants in an Italian landscape
Pen and brown ink and wash, signed, 9¾in by 13⅝in (24.7cm by 34.5cm)
Amsterdam DFl 44,080 (£9,731 : $15,570). 25.IV.83

ANTONIO CANALE called IL CANALETTO
A settee
Pen and brown ink and grey and brown wash over
black chalk, $9\frac{5}{8}$in by $7\frac{1}{2}$in (24.4cm by 19.1cm)
London £17,600($28,160). 18.XI.82

GIORGIO VASARI
The Rape of Ganymede
Pen and brown ink and wash heightened with
white over black chalk on blue paper,
$9\frac{1}{8}$in by $7\frac{1}{8}$in (23.1cm by 18cm)
London £12,100($19,360). 18.XI.82
Now in the Metropolitan Museum of Art,
New York

Following page
FRANCESCO MAZZOLA called IL PARMIGIANINO
Virgin and Child
Black chalk heightened with white, $10\frac{1}{4}$in by $7\frac{1}{4}$in (26.2cm by 18.4cm)
London £39,600($63,360). 18.XI.82

The drawing is a study for the *Madonna della Rosa*, now at Dresden, which was presented by
Parmigianino to Pope Clement VII in 1530, when he came to Bologna for the coronation of Charles V.
A. E. Popham has pointed out that the apparently motiveless action of the Virgin's right arm in the
painting is explained by the domestic atmosphere of this drawing: she is rolling up her sleeve to wash
the infant.

See over, page 39
FRANCESCO MAZZOLA called IL PARMIGIANINO
Study for a detail of a landscape
Black chalk, 11in by $8\frac{1}{2}$in (27.9cm by 21.5cm)
London £57,200($91,520). 18.XI.82

One of only six known landscape studies by Parmigianino, this drawing probably dates from his
early Roman period, *circa* 1524–25. The stitch holes along the left edge indicate that it was once part
of a sketchbook.

A sheet of studies by Albrecht Dürer

John Rowlands

Very few notable drawings by Albrecht Dürer remain in private hands, especially from the phase of his development before 1500, a time when the artist produced some of his most striking and imaginative designs. So the British Museum, already the possessor of one of the finest collections of Dürer drawings, is particularly fortunate to be able to acquire this important sheet of studies (Figs 1–2). It has been accepted in lieu of tax and allocated to the British Museum by the Minister for the Arts, on the recommendation of the Museums and Galleries Commission.

The drawing has been in Britain and possessed by notable collectors since the seventeenth century. It belonged to Sir Peter Lely, whose collector's mark is on the *recto* of the sheet. At his sale in April 1688 it was bought by the miniature painter William Gibson (*circa* 1644–1702/3). Gibson was a considerable purchaser at the sale and the price that he paid for this drawing has been written by him in the upper right-hand corner of the *recto*: *8* [s?] *3* [d?]. It subsequently belonged to the portrait painter Hugh Howard (1675–1757), who is chiefly remembered for his taste as a collector. He left his collection to his brother, the Bishop of Elphin, whose collection was kept together until 1873–74: the present sheet appeared in the sale at Sotheby's on 27 November 1874 as lot 39, and was bought by Lauser for the then substantial sum of £31. It was subsequently acquired in 1899 by G. Meyer and from him it entered the collection of Henry Oppenheimer, probably the most discerning collector of Old Master drawings active in the first half of the present century. Latterly it has been in the possession of a London private collector, who, at the time of the British Museum Dürer exhibition in 1971, deposited the drawing in the Department of Prints and Drawings, where it has remained ever since.

The sheet was produced while the artist was a journeyman, after the completion of his apprenticeship in the studio of Nuremberg's leading painter, Michael Wolgemut (1434–1519). Dürer later wrote of his apprenticeship in a memoir, saying, 'during that time God gave me diligence so that I learnt much, but I had to suffer a good deal from the journeymen'. He was evidently bullied for his precociousness by the older assistants, who probably found him a far from modest youth.

Although his precise steps cannot be traced, it is certain that his prime goal was the upper Rhineland, where he wandered in search of work from after Easter 1490 until after Whitsun 1494, when he returned home. He was particularly drawn to the region

The private treaty sale of this sheet of
sketches to the British Museum was
negotiated by Sotheby's.

Fig. 1
ALBRECHT DÜRER
*Virgin and Child seated at the foot of a tree
and other studies*
Verso: pen and brown ink, signed
with false monogram,
8⅛in by 7¾in (20.5cm by 19.7cm)
Reproduced courtesy of the
Trustees of the British Museum, London

Fig. 2
ALBRECHT DÜRER
Virgin and Child with drapery studies
Recto: pen and brown ink, signed with false
monogram and falsely dated *1519*,
8⅛in by 7¾in (20.5cm by 19.7cm)
Reproduced courtesy of the
Trustees of the British Museum, London

Fig. 3
Left
MARTIN SCHONGAUER
Christ as teacher
Pen and black ink, inscribed *das hat hubsch martin gemacht jm*
1469 jar, 8⅛in by 4⅞in (20.7cm by 12.4cm)
Reproduced courtesy of the
Trustees of the British Museum, London

Fig. 4
Opposite, left
ALBRECHT DÜRER
Holy Family
Recto: pen and brown ink, 8in by 8⅛in (20.4cm by 20.7cm)
Reproduced courtesy of the Universitätsbibliothek, Erlangen

Fig. 5
Opposite, right
ALBRECHT DÜRER
The Holy Family with the butterfly
Engraving, Meder A impression, 9¼in by 7¼in (23.6cm by 18.5cm)

by the presence there of Martin Schongauer (*circa* 1453–91), the leading engraver of the time and a considerable painter: Dürer greatly admired his work and wished to emulate it. Indeed, Schongauer cast a pervasive spell over many late Gothic engravers in Germany and the Low Countries, both at that time and in the years following his death. Unfortunately Schongauer died before Dürer could meet him, but the young artist was able, either then or a little later, to acquire some of his drawings. Two of these drawings, as it happens, are in the British Museum and one of them, *Christ as teacher* (Fig. 3), bears an inscription on the upper edge of the sheet in Dürer's hand, *das hat hubsch martin gemacht jm 1469 jar*. Despite its clear statement 'that fine [*hubsch* is used here as a synonym for *schön*] Martin has made this in the year 1469', many leading scholars have taken the view that it is a copy by Dürer after a work by Schongauer of 1469. There seems, however, no adequate reason for not taking Dürer's statement at its face value. The fact that a precise date is mentioned strongly suggests that Dürer obtained the drawing direct from the recently deceased artist's studio, which was run by his younger brother, Ludwig.

If the date is correct, Schongauer's drawing is an early one and it is instructive to compare the penwork with that in Dürer's sheet of early studies, especially in the representation of the drapery folds. Schongauer has worked with zest, but the penwork is more controlled than Dürer's; Schongauer is the creator of the style and his

draughtsmanship can be directly related to his work as an engraver. Dürer freely uses the vocabulary without having to consider such constraints. Indeed, his penwork has an unrestrained vigour that heralds a new-found freedom of expression.

All the same, among the drawings executed by Dürer during his years of travel as a journeyman, these studies reflect *hubsch* Martin's influence particularly strongly. Apart from the general stylistic links that have been noted already, this is apparent in the characteristic oval shape of the Virgin's face, with the large eyelids nearly closed.

The studies of the Virgin and Child, together with the contemporaneous and stylistically closely related drawing of the Holy Family in the University Library at Erlangen (Fig. 4), have been associated with Dürer's engraving, *The Holy Family with the butterfly* (Fig. 5). It is unlikely, however, that Dürer had this print in mind when he made the sketches, as the engraving is generally thought to have been executed about 1495, soon after the artist returned from his first visit to Italy. But he must have consulted either these studies, or others very like them, for the position of the Christ Child in his mother's arms.

The study of a left hand on the *verso* of the sheet in London may usefully be compared with the drawing on the *verso* of the Erlangen sheet. This bears an extraordinarily tense self portrait showing the highly strung young artist gazing out at us, supporting his head with his right hand. The study of the hand on the present sheet is further evidence of the artist's sensitivity of perception and delicacy of execution. Indeed, with experiment, Dürer was to develop the pen into his most effective and prolific means of expression. The distinction of the present sheet of studies is that it witnesses the first original steps that the young creative genius was making on this highly fruitful quest.

ANGLO-FLEMISH SCHOOL
Portrait of Edward VI as Prince of Wales
On panel, mid-sixteenth century, $37\frac{1}{2}$in by 30in (95.2cm by 76.2cm)
London £37,400 ($59,840). 11.VII.83
From the collection of the Lord Astor of Hever

ENGLISH SCHOOL
Portrait of Elizabeth I
On panel, *circa* 1575, 22$\frac{1}{2}$in by 17$\frac{1}{2}$in (57.1cm by 44.5cm)
London £28,600 ($45,760). 11.VII.83

RICHARD PARKES BONINGTON
Coast scene
On board, *circa* 1827, 6¾in by 10¾in (17.2cm by 27.3cm)
London £81,400 ($130,240). 6.VII.83

RICHARD PARKES BONINGTON
View in Venice, with the church of St George
On board, 12in by 16in (30.5cm by 40.6cm)
London £154,000 ($246,400). 2.III.83

Bonington was in Venice from 20 April to 19 May 1826 with his friend and patron
Baron Charles Rivet.

JOHN CONSTABLE, RA
View towards London from Putney, with St Paul's in the distance
On card laid down on board, 5¾in by 12½in (14.6cm by 31.7cm)
London £49,500 ($79,200). 6.VII.83

SIR EDWIN LANDSEER, RA
Blea Tarn looking south to Wetherlam, Cumberland
On panel, *circa* 1825–35, 8in by 10in (20.3cm by 25.4cm)
London £28,600 ($45,760). 6.VII.83
From the collection of the late Mrs M. J. A. Russell

This is one of a number of landscapes Landseer painted in Devon, the Lake District, Ireland and Scotland between 1825 and 1835.

Stratford Mill by John Constable, RA

Graham Reynolds

The full-size studies in oil which Constable made for his larger exhibition pictures are one of the more individual features of his art. He adopted the practice after he had moved permanently from Suffolk to London, on his marriage in 1816. Before that event he had been a regular visitor to his homeland. On his frequent visits to East Bergholt and Flatford he could paint his pictures in front of the motif, as with the *Boatbuilding near Flatford Mill*, or at any rate have constant recourse to the scene he was painting. He could no longer do this when the constraints of domestic life kept him in London. Yet his new responsibilities made him more ambitious than ever to make a mark at the Royal Academy. He chose to do this by sending pastoral landscapes of a size and style of handling that could not be overlooked. During a campaign spread over seven years, he selected subjects on the banks of the River Stour near Flatford and Dedham, which he painted on six-foot canvases. Since he was no longer in daily contact with these scenes, he had to rely on the small oil sketches and pencil drawings he had made earlier on the spot. These spontaneous notes of passing appearances had to be enlarged to the new scale, and the compositions had to be enlivened by the invention of incidents, by the introduction of trees and barges, and by formal devices such as altering the position of Dedham church tower. In that way, he aspired to combine the natural with the monumental and to attract attention on the crowded walls of the Summer Exhibition. To ensure that all the elements derived from earlier notes fitted into place, he worked out the new design on a canvas the same size as the exhibited picture. This full-size sketch would be painted with great verve, and its uncompleted nature gave him scope for experiment.

The White Horse, shown at the Academy in 1819 and now in the Frick Collection, New York, is the first significant example of Constable's concentration on studio composition. It also marks the first time, so far as we know, that Constable roughed out the composition on a canvas of the same size as the final version. This first full-scale sketch, in the National Gallery, Washington DC, is based on two oil sketches made from the bank opposite Willy Lott's house and a drawing in the sketchbook Constable carried about with him in 1814. These known preliminaries only provided part of the scene. The rest was invented or depended on sketches that have yet to be discovered. The full-size sketches for *The Hay Wain* and *The Leaping Horse*, respectively third and sixth in this series of large Stour subjects, are well known as they have hung together in the Victoria and Albert Museum since the 1860s. The big sketch for *View on the Stour near Dedham*, Constable's main Academy exhibit in 1822, is

Fig. 1
JOHN CONSTABLE, RA
Stratford Mill
Full-scale sketch, *circa* 1820, 51½ in by 72½ in (130.8cm by 184.2cm)
London £242,000 ($387,200). 6.VII.83
Now in the Yale Center for British Art, New Haven, Connecticut

Fig. 2
JOHN CONSTABLE, RA
Stratford Mill
Oil sketch of the left-hand side of
the composition, on panel, inscribed
and dated *17th August 1811*,
Stratford Oil Mill on the reverse,
$7\frac{1}{4}$in by $5\frac{3}{4}$in (18.3cm by 14.5cm)
Reproduced courtesy of
Adams Antiques

probably rather better known than the final version. It is at Royal Holloway College, Egham, which has been generous in allowing its inclusion in loan exhibitions. The exhibited picture is in the Huntington Art Gallery, San Marino, and not available for loan. Nor is the large sketch for *The Lock*, Constable's exhibit of 1824, particularly well known outside the Art Museum, Philadelphia, where it now hangs.

These sketches account for the formative stages of five out of the six large 'canal' scenes which Constable regarded as his most important contribution to British painting. The sixth of the series, known variously as *Stratford Mill* and *The Young Waltonians*, was his chief exhibit in 1820. It has been a matter of debate whether there is also a full-size oil sketch for this work.

A large oil answering to this description came to light some twenty-five years ago (Fig. 1), and was included by R.B. Beckett as an addendum to his typescript list of Constable's paintings. All that was known of its previous history was that it had been in the Wynn Ellis sale of 1876, an inconclusive provenance since that collection contained both genuine Constables and others now known to be false. On its re-emergence it attracted a good deal of sceptical appraisal; I myself was one of the disbelievers, influenced partly by the obviously false signature.

However, evidence has come to light which necessitates the full reconsideration of this canvas and puts its claims in a new and favourable light. An oil sketch of the left-hand side of the composition, hitherto unrecorded, came up for sale at Christie's on

Fig. 3
JOHN CONSTABLE, RA
Stratford Mill
Quarter-scale oil sketch, *circa* 1819–20, 12in by 16½in (30.5cm by 42cm)
From a private collection

19 November 1982. It was dated *17th August 1811* and quite evidently made on the spot (Fig. 2). On that particular summer day, Constable observed seven children playing at the mill, three of them with fishing rods. Various permutations of these young fishermen occur in other stages of the composition. A quarter-scale oil sketch shown at the Tate Gallery in 1971 retains the two right-hand figures in much the same attitudes, but the two on the left are apparently suppressed (Fig. 3). In the exhibited version the standing figure on the right has been replaced by two smaller children, and there is no sign of the fisherman originally sketched at the extreme left (Fig. 4). In the Wynn Ellis oil sketch there is a clear pentimento showing that the left-hand fisherman was originally included in this draft of the composition and subsequently painted out. The angle of the boy's rod is seen to be the same as in the sketch of 1811. Another pentimento shows that the angle of the rod held by the right-hand fisherman was originally more upright, a position which Constable adopted again in the exhibited version, though it is now a small kneeling boy who holds the rod. Other features which first appear in the full-scale sketch include the mill-wheel, the log

lying in the left-hand foreground, and the moorhen rising from the water in the right-hand foreground. The first two alterations are taken over into the final version, but not the moorhen, nor the girl leaning over the water below the waterwheel. She has also been carried over into the full-scale sketch from the small oil of 1811.

The Wynn Ellis sketch includes, as a component not seen in the earlier studies, the dead tree beyond the barge on the right-hand side of the composition. As Constable explained to David Lucas, this was an important part of the 'natural history' of the picture; the tree had been killed by the water's action on its roots. It suggested the nickname 'The touchwood tree', given to the painting by Constable's friend Arch-deacon John Fisher, who bought the exhibited picture for his solicitor John P. Tinney.

If the inscription *John Constable RA* in reddish-brown paint in the lower right-hand corner of the Wynn Ellis picture were to be taken seriously, it would imply that it had been produced, or at least reworked and signed, as a completed work after 1828, when Constable was belatedly elected a full Academician. But it is so unlike the form of Constable's genuine signatures, and so apparently a later addition to the surface, that it can be ignored as evidence. When the work itself is studied without this false clue, it can be seen to have the qualities which we should expect to find in a full-scale oil sketch for Constable's second large Stour scene. It incorporates, some-times in the form of discarded pentimenti, elements from the sketch made on the spot and the subsequent quarter-scale oil sketch, and it introduces for the first time other elements which are carried over into the final exhibited version. The assessment of its painterly qualities has been greatly assisted by the kindness of the owner of the exhibited picture, who allowed the two versions to be viewed side by side. That juxtaposition convinced me that the work now being discussed is indeed Constable's full-scale study for his 1820 exhibit at the Academy. The management of the water in the sketch is closely similar to passages in *The Hay Wain* and *View on the Stour near Dedham*. The waterlilies and posts, derived from drawings in the 1813 sketchbook, are paralleled in *The White Horse* and, later, in the *View on the Stour near Dedham*.

The canvas has been relined and unevenly cleaned, and there is at first sight a somewhat restless quality about the summary brushwork and the free impasto, which has been flattened in places. This has led to the suggestion that two hands may have worked on the canvas, or at least that Constable may have reworked the top surface at a date later than his under-painting. This explanation has been advanced to account for the bold slabs of impasto on the jackets of the fishing boys, the accents of light on the trees and other details left in an unfinished state. But I think that all these features are matched in the other large sketches, and that the criticism is based on a misunderstanding of Constable's methods and intentions in his full-size sketches. In the best description yet given of Constable's innovative technique, Basil Taylor pointed out that he rejected the established ideas of unity of notation and unity of touch: 'At some points the marks of the brush are quite descriptive . . . elsewhere there is only an evocative scribble suggesting general attributes of light and motion'. Even when he had introduced the extra delicacy and 'eyesalve' which he deemed necessary in an exhibited picture, his handling was severely criticized. Lawrence called his technique 'ferocious', and Count Forbin skied his paintings at the Paris Salon of 1824 because he thought, 'as the colours were rough they must be seen at a distance'. If this was true of his finished works, it is obvious that in making a

Fig. 4
JOHN CONSTABLE, RA
Stratford Mill
50in by 72in (127cm by 182.9cm)

This painting was exhibited at the Royal Academy in 1820 and is now in a private collection.

preparatory study, which he had no intention of showing to the public, he would be even more inventive and oblivious of conventional procedures for correct drawing.

For instance, even though the impasto on the sitting boy's jacket may seem reckless, it carries over the light and colour observed in 1811 and put into the quarter-scale sketch (Fig. 3); it reappears in the final version with a more refined touch, as befits an exhibition picture, and is closely similar to the treatment of the figures in the sketch for *The Leaping Horse*. Even so, he was no slave to method and varied his approach in each of his large oil sketches: that for *The Hay Wain* is broadly blocked in over a ground which plays a prominent part in its effect; that for *The Leaping Horse* is carried so far that at one time he intended it for the exhibited picture. Each was undertaken as a new experiment in artistic expression, and must be approached in an experimental frame of mind for fresh appraisal of his technique and inventive capabilities.

Constable regarded *Stratford Mill* as his most successful large Stour scene, 'grander' than *The Hay Wain*. It was the work by which he most wanted to be represented in loan exhibitions, and his constant, sometimes unsuccessful, attempts to prise it from its owner, John P. Tinney, embittered him. In view of the importance he attached to it, it is gratifying that the full-size sketch has been rediscovered. The later stages in the construction of all six of his Stour masterpieces are now accounted for.

JOHANN HEINRICH FUSELI, RA
The dismission of Adam and Eve from Paradise
59½in by 28½in (151.1cm by 72.3cm)
London £33,000($52,800). 10.XI.82

JOHANN HEINRICH FUSELI, RA
Eve, after the sentence and departure of the judge, despairing
59½in by 27½in (151.1cm by 69.8cm)
London £20,900($33,440). 10.XI.82

Both of these pictures were painted for Fuseli's Milton Gallery, which opened in Pall Mall on 20 May 1799.

PHILIP REINAGLE, RA and SAWREY GILPIN, RA
Portrait of Colonel Thomas Thornton
1796, 82in by 59in (208cm by 149.8cm)
New York $115,500(£72,188). 20.I.83
From the collection of the late Mrs Allan P. Kirby

Colonel Thornton was the most renowned sportsman of his day. Here he is shown stalking roebuck in the forest of Glen More, with the only twelve-barrelled rifle ever made.

GEORGE STUBBS, ARA
Hunter, Arab and water spaniel
39in by 48½in (99.1cm by 123.2cm)
London £275,000 ($440,000). 10.XI.82

JOHN BOULTBEE
A kennel huntsman letting his hounds out of the pen, with a view of Beeston Castle beyond
Signed and dated 1803, 27¾in by 35½in (70.5cm by 90.2cm)
London £30,800 ($49,280). 6.VII.83

MICHAEL 'ANGELO' ROOKER
Westminster Hall, London
Watercolour over pencil, signed and dated *177 . . .*, 14$\frac{3}{4}$in by 21in (37.5cm by 53.3cm)
London £25,300($40,480). 30.III.83

JOHANN HEINRICH FUSELI, RA
Massacre of the Innocents
Brushpoint and grey and brown wash over pencil, inscribed and dated *Roma 71 oct*, 17½in by 25¼in (44.4cm by 64.1cm)
London £41,800 ($66,880). 7.VII.83

On the *verso* is an unidentified scene of an assassin fleeing, in grey wash over pencil, inscribed and dated *Roma 74 april*.

RICHARD PARKES BONINGTON
Fishing
Watercolour with stopping out and traces of gum arabic, signed, early 1820s,
7in by 9¼in (17.8cm by 23.5cm)
London £33,000 ($52,800). 11.XI.82
From the collection of Dr William Brockbank

JOSEPH MALLORD WILLIAM TURNER, RA
Gibside, County Durham, the seat of the Earl of Strathmore
Watercolour, 10¼in by 17¼in (26.7cm by 43.8cm)
London £57,200 ($91,520). 7.VII.83

This watercolour, based on sketches made by Turner in 1817, was engraved by Samuel Rawle for
Robert Surtees's *History of the County of Durham*, Vol. II (1819).

SAMUEL THOMAS GILL
Monsieur Henri Noufflard's office
One of a series of eight watercolours, heightened with white and gum arabic,
signed with initials and dated '57, $6\frac{1}{2}$in by $9\frac{1}{2}$in (16.5cm by 24cm)
Melbourne total Aus $88,000 (£48,619: $77,790). 23.III.83

Henri Noufflard was a French wool merchant, who commissioned these
watercolours as a record of his residence in Sydney between 1855 and 1857.

JOSEPH STIELER
Portrait of Katharina Bozzaris
Circa 1841–45, 28in by 22½in (71.1cm by 57.1cm)
London £55,000 ($88,000). 1.VI.83

The subject was the daughter of the Greek revolutionary hero,
Marco Bozzaris.

Opposite
MARY ELLEN BEST
Dining table at the home of Dr Best
Watercolour, signed and dated *1838*, 10⅞in by 13⅞in (27.7cm by 35.3cm)
New York $13,200 (£8,250). 21.I.83
From the collection of Mrs Mary Sarg Murphy

This is one of over forty watercolours by the amateur painter
Mary Ellen Best sold last January in New York. The majority illustrate
the Yorkshire houses of the artist's family, Elmswell, Langton and
Howsham Halls.

JACQUES-JOSEPH TISSOT
A widow
Signed and dated *1868,* 27in by 19½in (68.6cm by 49.5cm)
New York $203,500 (£127,188). 24.II.83

This painting was exhibited at the Paris Salon of 1869.

SIMEON SOLOMON
Love in autumn
Signed with monogram and dated *Florence 1866*, 33in by 26in (83.8cm by 66cm)
New York $49,500 (£30,938). 28.X.82

JOHN ATKINSON GRIMSHAW
Nab Scar
On board, signed and dated *1864*, and titled, signed and dated on the backboard,
16in by 20in (40.6cm by 50.8cm)
London £55,000 ($88,000). 15.III.83

This is one of the finest of Grimshaw's early Lake District views, which were greatly influenced by the Pre-Raphaelite landscapes of Ford Madox Brown and John William Inchbold.

SIR LAWRENCE ALMA-TADEMA, RA
The kiss
On panel, signed and inscribed *Op. CCCXII*, 1891, 18in by 25in (45.7cm by 63.5cm)
London £55,000 ($88,000). 15.III.83

This painting was exhibited at the Royal Academy in 1892.

SIR EDWARD COLEY BURNE-JONES, Bt, ARA, RWS
The mirror of Venus
1867–77, 31in by 48in (78.8cm by 121.9cm)
London £143,000 ($228,800). 21.VI.83

The subject of this painting evolved from Burne-Jones's illustrations to William Morris's book *Earthly Paradise* (1868–70). A larger version of the picture was exhibited at the Grosvenor Gallery in 1877 and is now in the Gulbenkian Foundation, Lisbon.

RICHARD DADD
Contradiction: Oberon and Titania
Signed and dated *1854/1858*, and signed, titled and dated on
the reverse, 24in by 29¾in (61cm by 75.5cm)
London £550,000 ($880,000). 15.III.83

Dadd painted this picture while in Bethlem mental hospital (see
black and white illustration), for Dr William Charles Hood,
Physician Superintendent of the institution. It was previously
sold at Sotheby's on 18 March 1964 for £7,000.

Reproduced courtesy of the Bethlem Royal Hospital and the
Maudsley Hospital Health Authority

GEORGE VICAT COLE, RA
A Surrey cornfield
Signed and dated *1860*, 48in by 71in (121.9cm by 180.3cm)
London £29,150 ($46,640). 15.III.83

Opposite
HENRY NELSON O'NEIL, ARA
The parting cheer
Signed and dated *1861*, 52in by 74in (132cm by 188cm)
London £39,600 ($63,360). 15.III.83
This painting was exhibited at the Royal Academy in 1861.

The Art Journal reviewed the picture with enthusiasm, commenting: 'In *The parting cheer*, H. O'Neil
has written a great book, overflowing with the depth and dignity of human nature – a book that
requires to be read in detail, and most amply will it repay the labour.'

MYLES BIRKET FOSTER, RWS
Burnham Beeches
Watercolour heightened with bodycolour, signed with monogram, 8¼in by 13in (21cm by 33cm)
London £14,300 ($22,880). 21.VI.83

Figures in a field – *Winter work* by Sir George Clausen, RA

Kenneth McConkey

In 1880 a dispute raged in the Grosvenor Gallery in London. Contrary to the expectations of *The Spectator*, it did not centre around pictures by Holman Hunt or Burne-Jones, but rather around those of the young French painter, Jules Bastien-Lepage.[1] The centrepiece of his small retrospective within the gallery's summer exhibition was a large painting of exhausted field workers, *Les foins* (Fig. 1). Paintings of French peasants were not particularly unusual in London exhibitions at the time, but in this instance the field workers had been painted with amazing naturalistic exactness. In one swoop, Bastien-Lepage had conquered the capital of Pre-Raphaelitism and was effectively re-educating the rising generation of British artists to see nature with a plein-airiste's precision. One of the protagonists in the dispute was George Clausen, currently exhibiting a sophisticated interior scene of a woman dressed in black.[2] Having already been an admirer of John Robertson Reid's stern depiction of contemporary field labour, *Toil and pleasure* (Fig. 2), exhibited in the previous Royal Academy Summer Exhibition, Clausen was radically revising his ideas. The suave subjects of Whistler, Tissot and Gervex must give way to humbler themes representing rural rather than urban conditions. People must be depicted in an honest way, without artifice, as if one were encountering them in real life.

This simple, momentous realization changed Clausen's life. He moved out of London the following year to live at Childwick Green, near St Albans. He found it a 'liberation', because there 'one saw people doing simple things under good conditions of lighting . . . nothing was made easy for you: you had to dig out what you wanted.'[3] At the same time, Clausen completed his education in the new manner by spending two periods at the Académie Julien in Paris, and going on a painting expedition to Brittany. The first important result of this reorientation of style and subject matter was achieved in the winter of 1882–83 in the painting *Winter work*.

This picture was the result of numerous studies of field labourers preparing mangolds for sheep fodder. Rapid sketchbook notes (Figs 3–4) were supplemented by more detailed studies, aspiring, in the finished composition, to documentary exactness. The information gathering involved taking a series of photographs with the aid of a small glass-plate camera (Fig. 5). Like his French contemporary, Dagnan-Bouveret, Clausen used these instantaneous images to supplement, rather than replace, on-the-spot notes.[4] The grand naturalism which emerged was, therefore, a subtle assemblage

Fig. 1
Left
JULES BASTIEN–LEPAGE
Les foins
Signed, inscribed and
dated *DAMVILLERS,
1877, J. BASTIEN-
LEPAGE*, $70\frac{7}{8}$in by
$76\frac{3}{4}$in (180cm by
195cm)
Reproduced courtesy
of the Musée d'Orsay,
Paris

Fig. 2
Below
JOHN ROBERTSON REID
Toil and pleasure
Signed, 1879, 39in by
$71\frac{3}{4}$in (99cm by
182.2cm)
Reproduced courtesy
of the Tate Gallery,
London

Figs 3–4
SIR GEORGE CLAUSEN, RA
Two sketchbook pages with preparatory pencil drawings,
one measuring 6¾in by 4¼in (17.1cm by 10.7cm),
the other 7½in by 5in (19cm by 12.7cm)
Reproduced courtesy of the Royal Academy of Arts, London

Fig. 5
A field worker
A modern print from Clausen's 1¼in-
square glass-plate negative, *circa* 1883
Reproduced courtesy of the Royal
Photographic Society, Bath

Fig. 7
SIR GEORGE CLAUSEN, RA
Winter work
Signed, inscribed and dated *G. CLAUSEN 1883–4, CHILDWICK*, and signed, inscribed and dated
on the reverse, 30in by 35in (76.2cm by 88.9cm)
London £34,100 ($54,560). 3.XI.82

Now in the Tate Gallery, London

Fig. 6
Opposite
SIR GEORGE CLAUSEN, RA
December
On panel, signed, 9½in by 12in (24.1cm by 30.5cm)
From a private collection, the photograph reproduced courtesy of the Fine Art Society, London

Fig. 8
SIR GEORGE CLAUSEN, RA
Labourers after dinner
Signed and dated *1884*, 48in by 59$\frac{7}{8}$in (122cm by 152cm)
From a private collection

in which figures and setting were carefully contrived. In the process of achieving the final form of *Winter work*, the artist produced a small version of the subject, using only the two main labourers (Fig. 6), a secular up-to-date version of Millet's *Angelus*.[5]

Winter work was exhibited at the Grosvenor Gallery in 1883. While recognizing that this was a 'simple and honest' picture of 'labour in the fields', the critics were generally unprepared for its aggressive naturalism and preferred the more obviously pretty companion picture in the exhibition, *Haytime* (Art Gallery of Ontario, Toronto).[6] *The Times*, for instance, concurred with the implied criticism of the exhibition's hanging committee by remarking that the painting had been 'wisely skied'. 'It is true, of course, in a certain sense,' the critic grudgingly conceded, 'but it can give no pleasure . . . ', especially when compared with 'the other picture' of 'a girl dressed in white making hay'.[7]

Of greater significance is the fact that the artist himself felt that the composition of *Winter work* was incomplete, and during the next year he added the child with the hoop, at the right edge of the canvas (Fig. 7).[8] This addition lightened the rather sombre subject matter, without introducing an element of blatant narrative which might have been associated with Reid. Standing in the immediate foreground, almost touching the picture plane, the child articulates the space around the three other figures and heightens the spectator's consciousness of the dramatically centralized perspective. All at once, Reid's toilers begin to look artificial.

There can be no doubt that the daring of *Winter work* was enthusiastically received. It may have sparked off such works as James Guthrie's *A hind's daughter*, 1883 (National Gallery of Scotland, Edinburgh), and it forms part of the image community of many others like Edward Stott's *A French kitchen garden*, 1883 (Sheffield City Art Galleries). In these paintings there is a similar sense of spatial recession and a broad opaque painting across the forms in the rendering of the figure. But none of the comparable pictures by Clausen's contemporaries shares the ambition of *Winter work*. It alone attempted to portray the activities of a gang of labourers, to co-ordinate three or four figures 'doing simple things under good conditions of lighting'. Clausen returned to such problems in a more lyrical vein when he painted *Day dreams* in the summer of 1883, and he used the same female labourer for a stern portrait exhibited as *A woman of the fields* at the Liverpool Academy in the autumn of that year. The activities of the same peasant gang were observed in *Hoeing turnips*, 1884, and in the artist's Royal Academy picture of that year, *Labourers after dinner* (Fig. 8). This latter painting makes the debt to Bastien-Lepage's *Les foins* explicit. Indeed in all the paintings of the period, with the exception of head studies, the artist employed the 'depth of field' concept associated with Bastien. The eye is led from thickly painted foreground detail to the broad square handling of figures and beyond to the thin, blurred, almost impressionistic distance. This was the rustic naturalist mise-en-scène of the 1880s which was first fully employed in *Winter work*.

NOTES

1. For a study of Bastien-Lepage's influence in Britain, see Kenneth McConkey, 'The Bouguereau of the Naturalists, Bastien-Lepage and British Art', *Art History*, Vol. 1, no. 3, 1978, pp. 371–82

2. This picture was *La pensée*, now in the Glasgow Art Gallery and Museum. See Tyne and Wear and Bradford Museums, *Sir George Clausen RA, 1852–1944* (1980), exhibition catalogue by Kenneth McConkey. Until the publication of the author's monograph on Clausen, this catalogue remains the standard source of reference on the artist.

3. Sir George Clausen, 'Autobiographical Notes', *Artwork*, no. 25, spring 1931, p. 19

4. For reference to Pascal-Adolphe-Jean Dagnan-Bouveret's use of photography, see G.P. Weisberg, 'P.A.J. Dagnan-Bouveret and the Illusion of Photographic Naturalism', *Arts Magazine*, March 1982, pp. 100–15, and G.P. Weisberg, 'Making it Natural: Dagnan-Bouveret's Constructed Compositions for the Paris Salon of the 1880s', *The Scottish Art Review*, Vol. XV, no. 4, 1982, pp. 7–15. Weisberg has been the first to demonstrate that naturalist painters of the 1880s incorporated photography into the range of standard Beaux-Arts practices and that they did not simply transcribe photographs as latter-day Photo-realists might.

5. Clausen may well have painted *December* after *Winter work* had been exhibited; that is, the 'December' of the title may be that of 1883, rather than 1882. For further reference to this small oil, see *Clausen* (catalogue), pp. 38–39. Millet's *Angelus* was a currently controversial picture, which had been recently reproduced in *The Magazine of Art*, Vol. V, 1882, opp. p. 221. Beginning its review of *Winter work*, *The Times* referred to Clausen as one of the 'good students' of Millet. By the end of the 1880s the artist owned a series of etchings by Millet.

6. *The Magazine of Art*, Vol. VI, 1883, p. 352

7. *The Times*, 4 May 1883, p. 3

8. When he retouched a picture, to add to it or subtract from it, Clausen invariably extended the date. Thus, in this instance, the painting is inscribed, bottom left, *G. CLAUSEN 1883 – 4, CHILDWICK*.

RODERIC O'CONOR
View of Pont Aven
Signed and dated '99, 21½in by 25½in (54.6cm by 64.8cm)
London £20,900 ($33,440). 25.V.83

Opposite, above
HAROLD GILMAN
Kirkegaten, Flekkefjord
Signed, 1913, 19¾in by 24in (50.2cm by 61cm)
London £33,000 ($52,800). 25.V.83

Opposite, below
CHARLES GINNER, ARA
A corner in Chelsea
Signed, 1910, 38in by 53in (96.5cm by 134.6cm)
London £33,000 ($52,800). 25.V.83

SIR ALFRED MUNNINGS, PRA
Shade
Signed and dated *1911*, 24½in by 29½in (62.2cm by 75cm)
London £28,600 ($45,760). 3.XI.82
From the collection of the Art Gallery of New South Wales

LUCIAN FREUD, CH
Nude with dark hair (*Pregnant girl*)
1960–61, 34½in by 27½in (87.6cm by 69.8cm)
London £44,000 ($70,400). 25.V.83
From the collection of the late J. F. Parks

JACQUES-LOUIS DAVID
Belisarius and the child
1780, 25¼in by 30¼in (64.1cm by 76.8cm)
London £209,000 ($334,400). 21.VI.83

The subject matter of this painting was particularly popular after the publication of Marmontel's
Bélisaire in 1767. The moral tension inherent in the story, Justinian's great general reduced to beggary,
appealed to a number of late eighteenth-century French artists. David painted this picture in Rome,
brought it with him when he returned to Paris in 1780 and, the following year, painted a larger
version of the theme as his presentation piece for entry into the Académie. The larger work was
David's first major Neoclassical painting and its success at the Salon of 1781 established his reputation.

EUGENE DELACROIX
Notebook from a journey to Morocco
Fifty-six pages of notes and studies in watercolour, pen and ink and pencil, 26 January–2 March 1832, $3\frac{7}{8}$in by $6\frac{1}{2}$in (10cm by 16.5cm)
Monte Carlo FF 666,000 (£55,132:$88,211).
26.VI.83

Delacroix visited Morocco with the diplomatic mission of the Comte de Mornay in 1832. He was captivated by what he saw, writing to his friends Pierret and Villot on arrival: 'Rome n'est plus dans Rome . . . L'Antique n'a rien de plus beau . . . Je suis en ce moment comme un homme qui rêve et qui voit des choses qu'il craint de voir lui échapper.' He filled seven notebooks with his impressions, of which this is the first, and drew upon them for inspiration throughout his career.

JEAN-BAPTISTE-CAMILLE COROT
L'Italienne (*La juive d'Alger*)
Signed, *circa* 1870, 18½in by 14¾in (47cm by 37.5cm)
New York $715,000 (£446,875). 18.V.83
From the collection of the late Doris D. Havemeyer

GUSTAVE MOREAU
Desdemona
On panel, signed, *circa* 1875–78, 26¾in by 15½in (68cm by 39.3cm)
London £176,000($281,600). 21.VI.83

LUDWIG DEUTSCH
The fortune teller
On panel, signed and dated *Paris 1906*, $30\frac{3}{4}$in by $25\frac{1}{2}$in (78.1cm by 64.8cm)
New York $170,500 (£106,563). 26.V.83

JEAN BERAUD
On the boulevard, Paris
Signed, 25¼in by 31½in (64.1cm by 80cm)
London £143,000 ($228,800). 15.III.83

JOAQUIN SOROLLA Y BASTIDA
Two children on a beach, Valencia
Signed and dated *1904*, 29¾in by 41½in (75.5cm by 105.4cm)
London £94,600 ($151,360). 21.VI.83

FEDERICO ZANDOMENEGHI
Child with a bunch of flowers
Signed, 36¼in by 24⅜in (92cm by 62cm)
Florence L117,600,000 (£49,308:$78,893). 14.XII.82

IGNACIO ZULOAGA Y ZABALETA
Reclining maja with a macaw
Signed, 51¼in by 72½in (130.2cm by 184cm)
New York $137,500(£85,938). 24.II.83

This work was painted in Segovia in 1913.

WILLIAM-ADOLPHE BOUGUEREAU
Le guêpier
Signed and dated *1892*, 84in by 60in (213.3cm by 152.4cm)
New York $407,000 (£254,375). 26.V.83

This painting was exhibited at the Paris Salon of 1892.

MAX LIEBERMANN
The beer garden
Signed and dated *03*, 28⅛in by 39¾in (71.4cm by 101cm)
New York $209,000 (£130,625). 18.V.83

LOVIS CORINTH
Walchensee with three cows in a field
Signed and dated *1923*, 29in by 38¾in (73.7cm by 98.5cm)
London £61,600 ($98,560). 24.XI.82

EUGENE BOUDIN
Trouville: parasols on the beach
On panel, signed and dated 1886 *Trouville Août*, 9⅝in by 16⅛in (24.4cm by 41cm)
London £148,500 ($237,600). 1.XII.82

CLAUDE MONET
The River Zaan at Zaandam
Signed, 1871, 18¼in by 26in (46.3cm by 66cm)
New York $1,540,000 (£962,500). 18.V.83
From the collection of the late Doris D. Havemeyer

The Havemeyer Collection of Impressionist art

C. Hugh Hildesley

The impressive results of the auction of sixteen works from the collection of Henry Osborne and Louisine Waldron Elder Havemeyer, sold in New York by the executors of their daughter-in-law, Doris Dick Havemeyer, came as little surprise to the art world, which rarely witnesses the appearance of a group of Impressionist works of such consistent quality these days (Figs 1, 4–5 and pp. 84, 95, 102). A study of the background to the collection explains the particular attraction of the group.

In 1802, Henry Osborne Havemeyer's grandfather, Friedrich Christian Havemeyer (1774–1841), emigrated from Germany to New York, founding a bakery in Greenwich Village. Seven years later, in 1809, he started a sugar refinery in the same location. The business blossomed and was expanded by his son, Friedrich Christian Havemeyer, Junior (1807–91), and under Henry Osborne, born in 1847, the highpoint of the sugar fortune was reached. 'H.O.H.' developed a passion for collecting, bidding in New York salerooms under the unusual pseudonym of 'Mr Henry Henry', and concentrating much of his considerable means on the acquisition of Oriental works of art.

Meanwhile, in 1855, Louisine Waldron Elder was born in Philadelphia and grew up as a close family friend of the Cassatts. Mary Cassatt, eleven years senior to Louisine, had studied at the Pennsylvania Academy of the Fine Arts from 1861 to 1865 and had found the academic approach of that institution stifling to her artistic progress. In 1873, she settled in Paris, where, as she says: 'I had already recognized who were my true masters. I admired Manet, Courbet, and Degas. I hated conventional art. I began to live.' After a brief period under the classical tutelage of the academic painter Charles Chaplin at the insistence of her parents, Mary Cassatt broke away from tradition and allied herself with the new group of 'Independents'.

What more natural than for young Louisine to spend some time broadening her education in France? Thus in 1875, Louisine found herself in Paris, enrolled in a fashionable finishing school for young ladies, run by an Italian friend of Mary Cassatt's, one Madame del Sarte. Mary Cassatt clearly enjoyed the company of her young charge and performed her function *in loco parentis* by taking Louisine around the galleries and studios of her fellow artists.

Louisine described her first major purchase, at the insistence of her supremely well-qualified mentor, in her memoirs, *Sixteen to Sixty, Memoirs of a Collector*, printed

Fig. 1
EDGAR DEGAS
Au café-concert: 'La Chanson du Chien'
Gouache, pastel and monotype, signed, *circa* 1875–77, 24$\frac{3}{4}$in by 20$\frac{1}{8}$in (62.8cm by 51.1cm)
New York $3,410,000 (£2,131,250). 18.V.83
From the collection of the late Doris D. Havemeyer

Fig. 2
MARY CASSATT
Louisine Elder Havemeyer
Pastel, 1896, 29in by 24in (73.6cm by 61cm)
Reproduced courtesy of the
Shelburne Museum, Vermont

Fig. 3
The Havemeyer house,
1 East Sixty-sixth Street, by the architect
Richard Morris Hunt. The interior was
designed by Louis Comfort Tiffany with help
from Samuel Colman.

privately in 1961: 'I was almost sixteen years old when I first heard of Degas, of course through Mary Cassatt. She took me to see one of his pastels and advised me to buy it. How well I remember going with her to the color shop where it was for sale. Those color shops have launched more than one great artist, who later have made fortunes for dealers. The pastel was a 'Répétition de Ballet'. Old Plûque, the well-known *maître de ballet*, stood leaning upon his stick by the side scenes of the stage directing a rehearsal, the dancers were grouped about in various poses awaiting their turn while a *première* did a difficult *pas de deux* in the foreground. The drawing of the picture was as firm as a primitive, the difficulties of planes and perspective handled like a master, while the effect of light and shade and the beauty of color were simply entrancing. It was so new and strange to me! I scarce knew how to appreciate it, or whether I liked it or not, for I believe it takes special brain cells to understand Degas. There was nothing the matter with Miss Cassatt's brain cells, however, and she left me in no doubt as to the desirability of the purchase and I bought it on her advice.' Indulging in two months' spending allowance, one hundred dollars, Louisine embarked upon her lifelong career as a collector. The memoirs describe many subsequent purchases and often reveal her strong rapport with Degas's works. Mary Cassatt remained Louisine's close adviser, and later did her portrait (Fig. 2).

Fig. 4
EDOUARD MANET
Roses in a vase
Signed, 22in by 13¾in (55.8cm by 35cm)
New York $1,540,000 (£962,500). 18.V.83
From the collection of the late Doris D. Havemeyer

According to the catalogue of the posthumous 1884 Manet exhibition, this picture
was painted on 1 March 1883 , from flowers brought by Eugène Ephrussi.

Fig. 5
EDGAR DEGAS
L'attente
Pastel, signed, *circa* 1882, 19in by 24in (48.2cm by 61cm)
New York $3,740,000 (£2,337,500). 18.V.83
From the collection of the late Doris D. Havemeyer

Louisine Havemeyer wrote in her memoirs: 'The ballet interested the philosopher [Degas] perhaps more than any other subject during his working years . . . He preferred to portray the sinuous, sleek little creatures who came up from the heart of Paris with their mothers to present themselves at the opera and seek an entrance to the school which will enslave the best part of their young lives and make them the untiring pupils of "Plûque," the venerable *maître de danse*. You can see them to the life in a picture called *La famille Mante* or in one which I own, called *L'attente*.

'During a visit to Europe, Durand-Ruel allowed Mr Havemeyer to select a number of pictures from his private collection. It was this privilege which placed several of Degas's finest works in our collection. One is called *L'attente*. A ballet girl, waiting to be called, is seated upon a bench and is leaning down to tie her sandal . . . It is rather somber in tone and subject, but is the perfection of art in every detail.'

In 1883, Louisine married Henry Osborne Havemeyer and found herself in the fortunate position of joining one who shared her enthusiasm and was able to support it. A large town house, the interior designed by Louis Comfort Tiffany with help from Samuel Colman, was completed in 1892 (Fig. 3), and the Havemeyers moved into 1 East Sixty-sixth Street, at Fifth Avenue, and set about filling the massive structure with pictures, including possibly the leading Impressionist collection of the time.

The Havemeyer name has become inextricably linked with the Impressionist field, but Mary Cassatt also encouraged them to collect Old Masters, and accompanied them on an extended visit to Spain in 1901. The fruits of her encouragement were such works as El Greco's *Portrait of Cardinal Don Fernando Niño de Quevara* and the same artist's rare *View of Toledo*, Goya's *Majas on a balcony*, Rembrandt's *Portrait of the gilder, Herman Doomer*, Bronzino's *Portrait of a young man* and many others.

The Barbizon and Impressionist schools, however, held pride of place, and a brief listing of the Havemeyer holdings in these areas serves to describe the extraordinary nature of their collecting achievement: over one hundred and twenty works by Degas, forty-four by Courbet, twenty-eight by Monet, twenty-five by Corot, twenty-four by Manet, twenty by Mary Cassatt and eleven by Cézanne.

'H.O.H.' died in 1907 at the age of sixty. Louisine lived on with the collection until her death at the age of seventy-five in 1929. The majority of their paintings then passed by bequest to the Metropolitan Museum of Art, a gift described at the time by the Director, Dr Edward Robinson, as 'one of the most magnificent gifts ever made to a museum by a single individual'. After the gift, the Havemeyers' three children, Horace, Adaline and Electra, selected groups of works for themselves. The group sold this May was that chosen by Horace and his wife, Doris Dick.

It is interesting to observe that the gift of over two thousand works to the Metropolitan Museum was appraised in 1931 at $3,489,461, somewhat less than the price obtained for the single pastel, *L'attente*, by Degas in the recent auction (Fig. 5).

In analyzing the success of the sale, various factors emerge that reinforce some basic truths concerning the art market. The majority of the paintings had not been seen since 1929, with the exception of an occasional loan to a specialist exhibition, and this enhanced their appeal to an art market ever eager to find quality material that has not been in recent circulation. Moved only a few times since their creation, the Havemeyer paintings were also in extraordinarily fine condition, a much sought-after criterion of value.

Mary Cassatt's advice provides another clue to the unique quality of the Havemeyer Collection. Maintaining close contact with the Henry Osborne Havemeyers, both in person and through a voluminous correspondence, the artist firmly inculcated her taste into the developing connoisseurship of her friends, leading them systematically to the finest works available at the time and introducing them to the dealer Paul Durand-Ruel, a pivotal figure in the creation of their collection.

Finally, the provenance of these paintings naturally added to their lustre. There was a sense that this might be the last chance to acquire works collected by two of the first American collectors in the Impressionist field. For the Havemeyers, together with Mrs Potter Palmer in Chicago, can claim a considerable portion of the credit for making American collectors aware of the importance of the Impressionist movement.

PAUL CEZANNE
Flowers in a vase
Circa 1885, $18\frac{1}{4}$in by $21\frac{7}{8}$in (46.3cm by 55.5cm)
New York $2,090,000 (£1,306,250). 18.V.83
From the collection of the late Doris D. Havemeyer

EDGAR DEGAS
Rearing horse
Bronze, signed, numbered $\frac{4}{7}$ and stamped with the foundry mark *A. A. Hébrard Cire Perdue*,
circa 1870–81, height 12in (30.5cm)
New York $121,000(£75,625). 4.XI.82
From the collection of Mrs Walter Buhl Ford II

MARY CASSATT
Baby John being nursed
Pastel on canvas, signed, 1910, 32in by 25½in (81.3cm by 64.8cm)
New York $385,000 (£240,625). 18.V.83

PIERRE-AUGUSTE RENOIR
Bather
Signed and dated *91*, $31\frac{7}{8}$in by $25\frac{3}{8}$in (81cm by 64.4cm)
New York $2,750,000(£1,718,750). 18.V.83

THEO VAN RYSSELBERGHE
Regatta
Signed with monogram and dated *1892*, 25¼in by 33in (64.1cm by 83.8cm)
New York $198,000(£123,750). 19.V.83
From the collection of the late Hugo Perls

The painted wood frame was executed by Henry van de Velde.

RAOUL DUFY
Regatta at Trouville
Signed, 1907, 19¾in by 31½in (50.1cm by 80cm)
New York $341,000 (£213,125). 18.V.83

EDOUARD MANET
Study for 'Le déjeuner à l'atelier'
Pen and brush and brown ink, signed with initials, 1868, 8⅛in by 6⅝in (20.6cm by 16.7cm)
London £34,100 ($54,560). 23.III.83
From the collection of Mrs G. B. Springell

This is a study for two of the figures in Manet's composition *Le déjeuner à l'atelier*, in the
Bayerische Staatsgemäldesammlungen, Munich.

PABLO PICASSO
Costume design for Léonide Massine as the Chinese Conjurer in 'Parade'
Pen and brown ink, signed, 1917, 10¾in by 7¾in (27.3cm by 19.7cm)
London £11,000 ($17,600). 9.VI.83

Parade, with libretto by Jean Cocteau, music by Eric Satie and choreography by Massine, was first performed by Diaghilev's Ballets Russes in Paris on 18 May 1917, and marked Picasso's debut as a stage designer.

PABLO PICASSO
Still life with classical head and bunch of flowers
Watercolour, pen and brush and indian ink, signed and dated *3 juillet XXXIII*,
15⅛in by 19¼in (38.3cm by 48.9cm)
London £121,000 ($193,600). 1.XII.82
From the collection of the Edward James Foundation, West Dean, Sussex

PABLO PICASSO
Head of a woman
On board, signed, 18½in by 12½in (47cm by 31.7cm)
New York $1,375,000(£859,375). 18.V.83

This picture was painted in Paris in 1901.

PABLO PICASSO
Pots and lemon
1907, 21¾in by 18in (55.2cm by 45.7cm)
London £231,000 ($369,600). 29.VI.83

This picture dates from the summer of 1907, shortly after Picasso had completed his pioneering Cubist work *Les demoiselles d'Avignon*. The drawing opposite could be a study for the figure on the far right in that painting, or for the slightly later *Nu à la draperie*.

PABLO PICASSO
Nez quart de Brie
Pencil on paper laid down on board, 1907, 12¼in by 9⅜in (31.1cm by 23.8cm)
New York $187,000 (£116,875). 4.XI.82
From the collection of the late Mr and Mrs Georges E. Seligmann

PABLO PICASSO
Head of a woman
Red and black chalk, signed and dated *8–21*, 25¼in by 19⅜in (64.1cm by 49.2cm)
New York $286,000 (£178,750). 18.V.83
From the collection of the Metropolitan Museum of Art, New York

GIORGIO DE CHIRICO
Trophy
Pastel, signed and dated *1926*, 41⅜in by 29⅜in (105.1cm by 74.6cm)
London £85,800 ($137,280). 23.III.83

PAUL KLEE
Geschwister
Signed, and signed, titled, dated and numbered *1930 E.8* on the stretcher,
27¾in by 17¾in (70.5cm by 45.1cm)
New York $467,500 (£292,188). 18.V.83
From the collection of the late Mrs G. David Thompson

WASSILY KANDINSKY
Nude
Signed and dated *1911*, 59in by 37¾in (149.8cm by 95.9cm)
New York $1,100,000 (£687,500). 4.XI.82
From the collection of Mr and Mrs Frederick Weisman

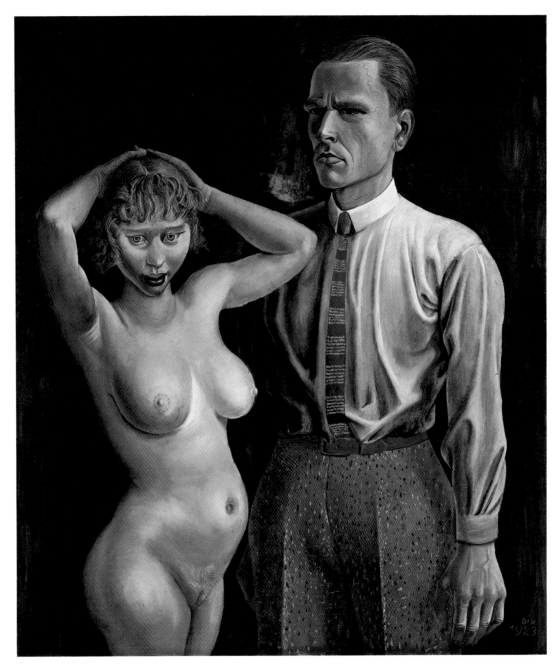

OTTO DIX
Self portrait with model
Signed and dated *1923*, and signed, titled and dated on the reverse,
41⅜in by 35½in (105.1cm by 90.2cm)
London £220,000 ($352,000). 29.VI.83

EGON SCHIELE
Portrait of Dr Rieger
Watercolour, gouache and pencil, signed and dated *1917*,
17½in by 11¼in (44.5cm by 28.5cm)
London £77,000 ($123,200). 29.VI.83

Dr Heinrich Rieger, a dentist, was one of the earliest collectors of Schiele's work.

JOAN MIRO
Nocturne
Gouache and oil wash on paper, signed, and signed, titled, numbered *12* and dated *Palma de Majorque 2/XI/1940* on the reverse, 15in by 18⅛in (38.1cm by 46cm)
London £297,000 ($475,200). 23.III.83

This work is the twelfth in a series of twenty-three *Constellations* executed between January 1940 and September 1941. Miró described the genesis of the series in a letter to Roland Penrose: 'After my work [on oil paintings] I dipped my brushes in petrol and wiped them on the white sheets of paper from the album, with no pre-conceived ideas. The blotchy surface put me in a good mood and provoked the birth of forms, human figures, animals, stars, the sky, and the moon and the sun . . . Once I had managed to obtain a plastic equilibrium and bring order among all these elements, I began to paint in gouache, with the minute detail of a craftsman and a primitive.'

HENRY MOORE, OM, CH
Draped figures in a shelter
Coloured chalk, pen and ink, and watercolour heightened with white, signed and dated *41*,
12½in by 21½in (31.7cm by 54.6cm)
London £39,600($63,360). 1.XII.82
From the collection of Lady Huxley

WILLIAM MERRITT CHASE
Afternoon in the park
Pastel on paper laid down on canvas, signed, *circa* 1889, 19in by 15¼in (48.2cm by 38.7cm)
New York $308,000 (£192,500). 2.XII.82
From the collection of the late Charlotte V. Bergen

This is a portrait of the artist's wife, Alice, in Prospect Park, Brooklyn.

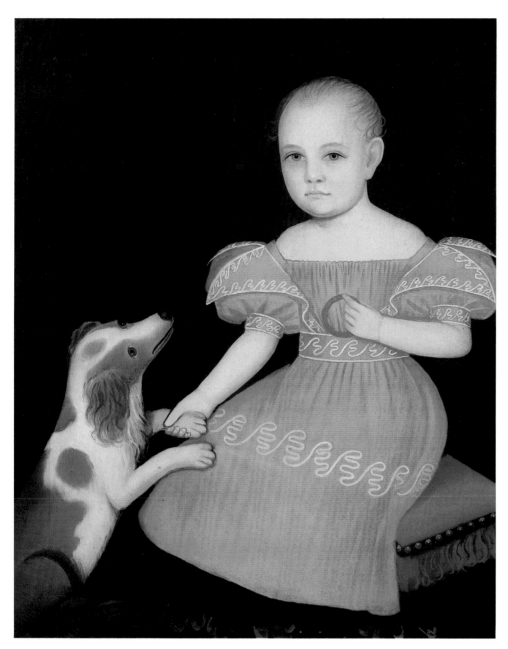

AMMI PHILLIPS
Child in pink with her spaniel
31in by 25in (78.7cm by 63.5cm)
New York $137,500 (£85,938). 2.VI.83

WINSLOW HOMER
A sharpshooter on picket duty
Signed and dated '63, 12¼in by 16½in (31.1cm by 41.9cm)
New York $352,000 (£220,000). 22.X.82
From the collection of Mrs Alexander McWilliams

This is the original painting for the well-known wood engraving *The Army of the Potomac – A sharpshooter on picket duty*, published in *Harper's Weekly*, 15 November 1862. The painting, Homer's earliest adult work in oil, was completed in the latter part of 1862 from sketches taken during a period as an artist correspondent for *Harper's*, while the artist was with General McClellan's Army of the Potomac, encamped near Yorktown, Virginia, in October 1861.

ALBERT BIERSTADT
The last of the buffalo
Signed, *circa* 1888, 26in by 36in (66cm by 91.5cm)
New York $792,000 (£495,000). 2.VI.83

The painting focuses on the central theme of Bierstadt's two larger versions of this subject. The artist commented on his buffalo pictures that he 'endeavored to show the buffalo in all his aspects, and depict the cruel slaughter of a noble animal now almost extinct'. In fact, *The last of the buffalo* helped to bring the plight of the animal to national attention, and the ensuing public outcry resulted in the first official census.

Frederic Remington's *The Norther*

Michael Edward Shapiro

The sale of Frederic Remington's *The Norther* (Fig. 1) marked the rediscovery of one of the artist's rarest sculptures, a work that signified his brilliant introduction to the lost-wax method and began his long association with the foundry called the Roman Bronze Works. Before the Sotheby's sale, *The Norther* was known by a single casting in the collection of the Gilcrease Institute in Tulsa, Oklahoma (Fig. 2). The bronze that was auctioned at Sotheby's and acquired by the National Cowboy Hall of Fame and Western Heritage Center in Oklahoma City, Oklahoma, was located in the collection of descendants of Grant Barney Schley, who had acquired it from the artist in 1900.

The sculpture depicts a cowboy and his horse being buffeted from the rear by fierce winds. The horse, with his four hooves firmly planted on the ground, his head lowered and eyes narrowed to protect himself from the storm, has a thick winter coat, whose matted and wind-blown surfaces are evoked by richly textured and inflected bronze (Fig. 3). The cowboy, whose smooth leather jacket contrasts with the horse's striated coat, peers into the distance from beneath a hat secured under his chin and wears deeply undercut chaps, whose form resembles the horse's tail and mane.

When Remington began his model for this sculpture early in 1900, he had already produced four sculptures: *The bronco buster*, 1895; *The wounded bunkie*, 1896; *The wicked pony*, 1898, and *The scalp*, 1898. These sculptures, which like *The Norther* consist of a horse and rider, were expertly cast at the Henry–Bonnard Bronze Foundry in New York by the sand-casting method. They have the smooth, highly polished and reflective forms characteristic of that method of casting. However, the sand process could not duplicate the gritty textures of Western life, the details of rocks, chaps and fur which Remington included in his illustrations and paintings, and which he wished his sculptures to possess as well.

In contrast to the animated forms and smooth surfaces of his first four sculptures, *The Norther* signified Remington's endorsement of the lost-wax process and represented the artist's rapid exploration of its ability to duplicate a deeply undercut and richly textured model with absolute fidelity. So enamoured did Remington become with this method that from *The Norther* onwards he relied on the Roman Bronze Works, New York, the first American foundry dedicated to this process, to cast all of his sculptures. Stimulated and encouraged by Riccardo Bertelli, head of the foundry, Remington in his subsequent bronzes combined his passion for movement with deeply inflected and crisply cast surfaces.

Fig. 1
FREDERIC REMINGTON
The Norther
Bronze, signed, stamped with the foundry mark *Cire Perdue Cast Roman Bronze Wks. N.Y.* twice and
EG CAST on the base, and dated *Copyrighted 1900*, height 22 in (56 cm)
New York $715,000 (£446,875). 22.X.82

Fig. 2
FREDERIC REMINGTON
The Norther
Bronze, height 22 in (56 cm)
Reproduced courtesy of the
Gilcrease Institute, Tulsa, Oklahoma

Unpublished entries in the artist's account books in the Remington Art Museum, Ogdensburg, New York, suggest that the sculptor was working on his model in early March of 1900, that he was paying particular attention to the sculpture's surface, and that he was considering naming the sculpture either *The blizzard* or *The Norther*. By the time he copyrighted his model on 30 June 1900, he had decided on the latter title.

In a letter of 16 July 1902 (in the Metropolitan Museum of Art Library), Remington briefly described his most important artistic achievements and stated that three casts of *The Norther* had been made. The date of the letter provides us with a *terminus ante quem* for the casting of the series, and its text refers to the owners of the three casts. Remington wrote:

The Norther 3 copies – owned by Schley – and another in Cleveland Ohio + Cobby[?] of Orange –

The cast that was sold at Sotheby's is the cast that Remington identified as 'owned by Schley', since it remained in the Schley family until its auction last year. In fact, Remington used a letter 'S' as the brand on the horse, as a conceit on the initial of the sculpture's owner. Unfortunately, the circumstances of the sculpture's sale to Grant Barney Schley are not yet known, but the listing of the Schley cast first in the artist's letter, and the placing of what looks like a small number '1' in the 'F' of the artist's signature on the base of this cast, suggest that the Schley cast may well have been the first of the three casts produced and therefore the first lost-wax casting by Remington. The Schley casting is additionally rare for the inscription of one of the key foundrymen at the Roman Bronze Works, Eugene Gargani, who placed his initials on the base in an act which indicates the Schley cast to be a triumphant combination of the skills of both artist and founder.

Since the sale of the Schley bronze, the third cast of *The Norther* has appeared from a private collection in Cleveland. This is probably the cast which Remington referred to in his Metropolitan Museum letter as 'in Cleveland Ohio', and it is now on long-term loan to the Cleveland Museum of Art. The cast in the Gilcrease Institute is probably the one listed by Remington as belonging to 'Cobby[?] of Orange', and if this is so all three casts of the sculpture are now accounted for.

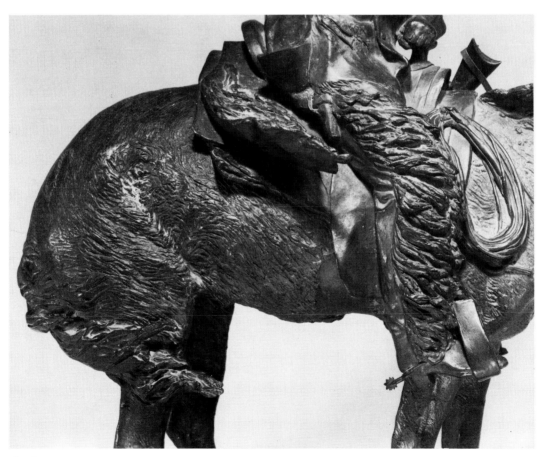

Fig. 3
Detail of Fig. 1

Fig. 4
FREDERIC REMINGTON
The bronco buster
Signed, *circa* 1895, 35in by 23in (88.9cm by 58.4cm)
New York $473,000 (£295,625). 2.VI.83

The theme of this painting is the same as that which Remington used for his first
and most popular bronze, also entitled *The bronco buster*, although the composition
is different. The bronze was conceived in 1894 and first executed in 1895.

Fig. 5
FREDERIC REMINGTON
The herd boy
Signed, *circa* 1909, 27 in by 45 in (68.5 cm by 114.3 cm)
Reproduced courtesy of the Museum of Fine Arts, Houston, Texas
(Hogg Brothers Collection)

Many of Remington's sculptures are closely related to paintings and drawings (Fig. 4), and *The Norther* is no exception. *Drifting before the storm* (unlocated) is a painting that depicts two riders herding cattle in the midst of a snowstorm. The lead rider has his hat fastened under his chin and is clad against the wind, which blows against him like the cowboy in the sculpture. *The herd boy, circa* 1909 (Fig. 5), in the Museum of Fine Arts, Houston, duplicates the wind-blown atmosphere and the static pose of *The Norther*, but exchanges the figure of the cowboy for an Indian. The subject and pose of the painting show that the configuration Remington devised in 1900 for a sculpture was adapted and reused almost a decade later in a different medium.

Remington's first sculpture, *The bronco buster*, pitted man against his steed, but in *The Norther* horse and rider are combined as they endure forces beyond their control. The horse and rider, so eloquently still in *The Norther*, suggest the combined will of man and animal to endure, and possibly triumph over, adversity. Like any great work of art, *The Norther* makes a statement about the artist and the culture in which he existed. In this instance we have examined Remington's first lost-wax bronze and how he exploited the technical limitations of the method to create a work which constituted a turning point in his career as a sculptor. It not only expresses the waning days of the frontier and the combative personality of the artist himself, but also raises questions about human isolation, endurance, the will to survive and, on a political level, the fears and concerns of Americans at the turn of the century.

MARTIN JOHNSON HEADE
Hummingbird and passion flowers
16in by 20in (40.6cm by 50.8cm)
New York $104,500 (£65,313). 22.X.82

Opposite, above
JASPER FRANCIS CROPSEY
Greenwood Lake
Oil on canvas laid down on panel, signed and dated *1870*, 38¼in by 68¼in (97.2cm by 173.2cm)
New York $286,000 (£178,750). 2.VI.83
From the collection of the Seneca Falls Central School District, New York

Opposite, below
JOHN FREDERICK KENSETT
On the coast
Signed with monogram and dated *'70*, 18¼in by 30in (46.3cm by 76.2cm)
New York $269,500 (£168,438). 2.VI.83

CHARLES SHEELER
Classic landscape
Signed and dated *1931*, 25in by 32¼in (63.5cm by 81.9cm)
New York $1,870,000 (£1,168,750). 2.VI.83
From the collection of the Edsel and Eleanor Ford House, Detroit

Sheeler's fascination with industrial landscape developed after a commission from Henry Ford to photograph his River Rouge factory. The photographs received worldwide attention and praise, encouraging the artist to create a series of paintings, including *Classic landscape*. He later explained his stylistic aims in this period: 'I had come to feel that a picture could have incorporated in it the structural design implied in abstraction and be presented in a wholly realistic manner.' The abstract realism and solid geometry of industrial forms in *Classic landscape* make it an important example of American Precisionist painting.

CHARLES SHEELER
Tulips
Conté crayon, signed twice and dated *1931*, 29½in by 22½in (74.9cm by 57.1cm)
New York $209,000 (£130,625). 2.VI.83

This is one of a group of 'portraits' that Sheeler made of his photography studio, which illustrate the close relationship between his paintings and his photographs.

CY TWOMBLY
Untitled
Oil and pencil on canvas, signed and dated *NY 1968* on the reverse,
68⅛in by 87⅞in (173cm by 223.2cm)
London £55,000 ($88,000). 2.XII.82

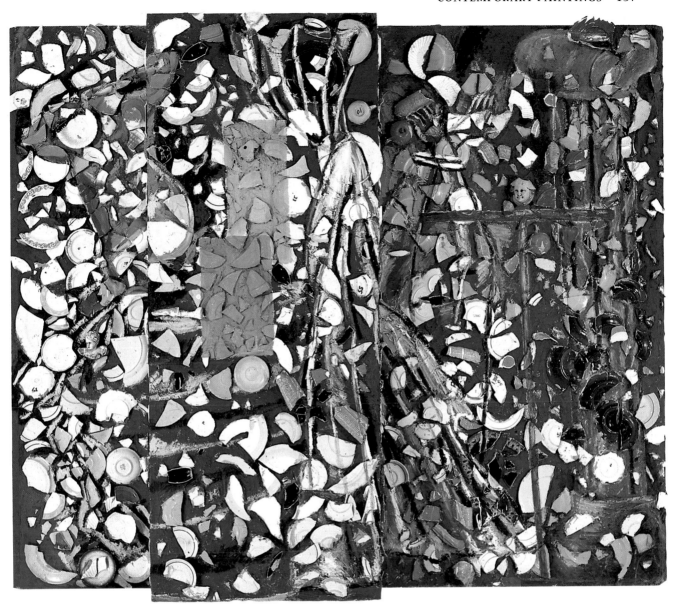

JULIAN SCHNABEL
Notre Dame
Oil, wax and plates on panel, signed and dated *1979* on the reverse,
90in by 108in by 12in (228.6cm by 274.2cm by 30.5cm)
New York $93,500 (£58,438). 20.V.83

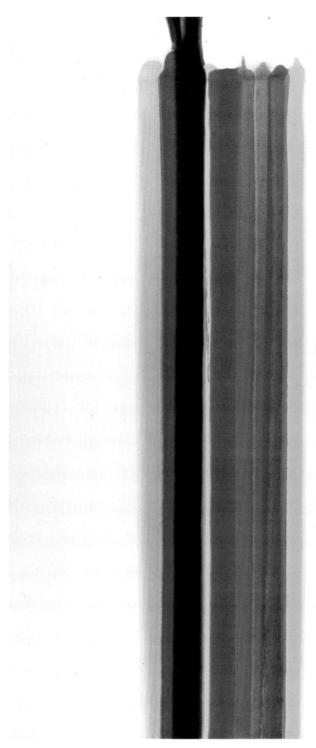

MORRIS LOUIS
Pillar of celebration
Magna on canvas, signed, titled and dated *1961* on the stretcher,
88¾in by 55in (225.5cm by 139.7cm)
New York $242,000 (£151,250). 20.V.83
From the collection of Vincent Melzac

JASPER JOHNS
In memory of my feelings – Frank O'Hara
Oil on canvas with objects, signed, titled and dated *61*, 40in by 60in (101.6cm by 152.4cm)
New York $363,000 (£226,875). 20.V.83
From the collection of Dr and Mrs Eugene A. Eisner

HANS HOFMANN
X
Signed and dated *55*, 60in by 48in (152.4cm by 121.9cm)
New York $121,000 (£75,625). 9.XI.82

ALEXANDER CALDER
Little tinkle
Mobile stabile, painted metal, 1938, length 50in (127cm)
London £67,100 ($107,360). 29.VI.83

NICHOLAS CHEVALIER
Mount Zero and Lake Taylor, Victoria
Signed and dated *1862*, 31⅛in by 48¼in (79cm by 122.5cm)
Melbourne Aus $176,000 (£97,238:$155,581). 23.III.83

This was one of Chevalier's most popular and successful works. Shortly after its appearance, the *Illustrated Melbourne Post*, noted: 'The composition and finish of this most attractive picture are equally excellent, and M. Chevalier has shown that the pencil of the true artist can produce for Australia, landscapes not unworthy of comparison with the most lovely portions of the old world.'

THOMAS WILLIAM BOWLER
Simonstown from Kalk Bay
Watercolour over pencil heightened with white, signed and dated *1865*,
7⅞in by 18½in (20cm by 47cm)
London £3,740 ($5,984). 13.X.82
From the collection of Mr R. Lewis

ROBERT GWELO GOODMAN
Hermanus
Signed with initials, 32¼in by 46⅞in (82cm by 119cm)
Johannesburg R 25,000 (£14,535: $23,256). 17.V.83
From the collection of Mr and Mrs Arnold Rosenberg

FERNANDO BOTERO
The family
Signed and dated *68*, 74in by 71in (188cm by 180.3cm)
New York $176,000 (£110,000). 23.XI.82

RUFINO TAMAYO
The astrologers of life
Signed and dated *0–47*, 80in by 60in (203cm by 152.4cm)
New York $96,250 (£60,156). 23.XI.82
From the collection of the late Donald Kellogg

Prints

MARTIN SCHONGAUER
Christ before Annas
Engraving, 6½in by 4½in (16.4cm by 11.5cm)
London £10,780 ($17,248). 17.VI.83

ALBRECHT DÜRER
Joachim and the angel
One print from a volume containing the *Three Large Woodcut Series* (the *Life of the Virgin*,
the *Large Passion* and the *Apocalypse*), 1511 edition, in a later sixteenth-century
gilt-stamped vellum binding with the insignia of the Stadtbibliothek, Nuremberg,
sheet size $17\frac{1}{8}$in by $11\frac{7}{8}$in (43.4cm by 30.1cm)
London total £222,200 ($355,520). 17.VI.83

REMBRANDT HARMENSZ. VAN RIJN
Jupiter and Antiope
Etching, smaller plate, second state, *circa* 1631, $3\frac{1}{4}$in by $4\frac{1}{2}$in (8.4cm by 11.3cm)
New York $19,800 (£12,375). 19.XI.82

ROBERT HAVELL JR after JOHN JAMES AUDUBON
Trumpeter swan
Hand-coloured etching, engraving and aquatint, 1838, from *Birds of America*,
25½in by 38in (64.7cm by 96.5cm)
New York $45,100 (£28,188). 16.VI.83

Opposite
GIOVANNI DOMENICO TIEPOLO
The Flight into Egypt
One of a set of twenty-seven etchings, second state, 1753, sheet size 10⅜in by 15½in (26.5cm by 39.5cm)
London £14,850 ($23,760). 17.VI.83

THOMAS SUTHERLAND after JOHN FREDERICK HERRING SR
Memnon, winner of the Great St Leger Stakes at Doncaster, 1825
Hand-coloured aquatint partially printed in colours, published 1825, 15⅜in by 19¾in (39cm by 50.3cm)
London £825 ($1,320). 17.VI.83

Opposite
EDGAR DEGAS
Self portrait
Etching, second state, 1857, 9⅛in by 5⅝in (23.1cm by 14.4cm)
London £39,600 ($63,360). 16.VI.83

EDVARD MUNCH
By the deathbed
Lithograph on green laid paper, signed, 1896, 16in by 19¾in (40.5cm by 50.3cm)
London £69,300 ($110,880). 16.VI.83

The death of Munch's sister, Sophie, provided the inspiration for this print.

ODILON REDON
Béatrice
Lithograph printed in colours, trial proof, 1897, 13¼in by 12¼in (33.6cm by 31cm)
New York $46,200(£28,875). 18.XI.82

PABLO PICASSO
Bust of woman in a hat
Linoleum cut printed in colours, signed and numbered *28/50*, 1962,
24¾in by 20⅞in (63cm by 53cm)
New York $53,900 (£33,688). 5.V.83

PABLO PICASSO
Portrait of Fernande Olivier
Drypoint, 1906, 6$\frac{3}{8}$in by 4$\frac{5}{8}$in (16.2cm by 11.8cm)
New York $71,500 (£44,688). 17.XI.82

There are only three other known impressions of this drypoint of Picasso's mistress. It was part of a sale of prints from the estate of the artist, inherited by his granddaughter Marina Picasso.

Photographs

NICEPHORE NIEPCE
Cardinal Amboise
Heliogravure, 1826, printed 1864, $6\frac{1}{4}$in by $5\frac{1}{8}$in (16cm by 13cm)
London £3,520($5,632). 29.X.82

WILLIAM HENRY FOX TALBOT
Trafalgar Square during the construction of Nelson's Column
Talbotype, late 1843, $7\frac{1}{4}$in by $8\frac{7}{8}$in (18.5cm by 22.5cm)
London £7,480($11,968). 29.X.82

LOUIS ROBERT
The park at St Cloud
Albumen print from waxed-paper negative, *circa* 1850–55, 12⅝in by 10⅛in (32.1cm by 25.8cm)
London £3,080 ($4,928). 25.III.83

FORTUNATO DEPERO
Message with self portraits
Three self portraits on separate sheets, with messages
on *recto* and *verso* in red and black tempera, and a Futurist
envelope, 1915, each approx. 3¼in by 3in
(8.2cm by 7.6cm)
New York $11,825 (£7,391). 9.XI.82

This was one of a collection of Futurist photographs formed
by the late Giovanni Lista.

FLORENCE HENRI
Still life with pear and lemon
Silver print, with photographer's stamp
on the reverse, 1923, probably printed
mid-1950s,
11in by 9¼in (27.9cm by 23.5cm)
New York $3,410 (£2,131). 10.V.83
From the collection of Romeo Martinez

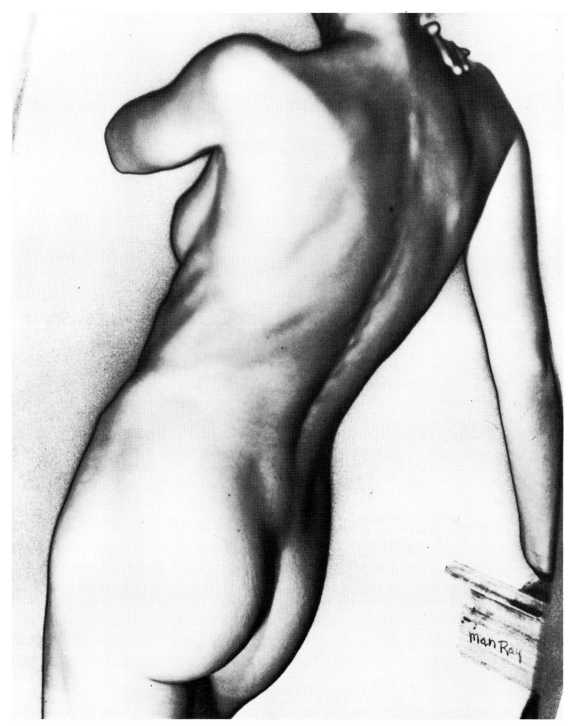

MAN RAY
Nu de dos (*Juliet*)
Solarized silver print, signed, with the studio stamp on the reverse, 1930s, printed *circa* 1946,
13in by 10in (33cm by 25.4cm)
New York $12,650 (£7,906). 11.V.83
From the collection of John Kasmin

Manuscripts and printed books

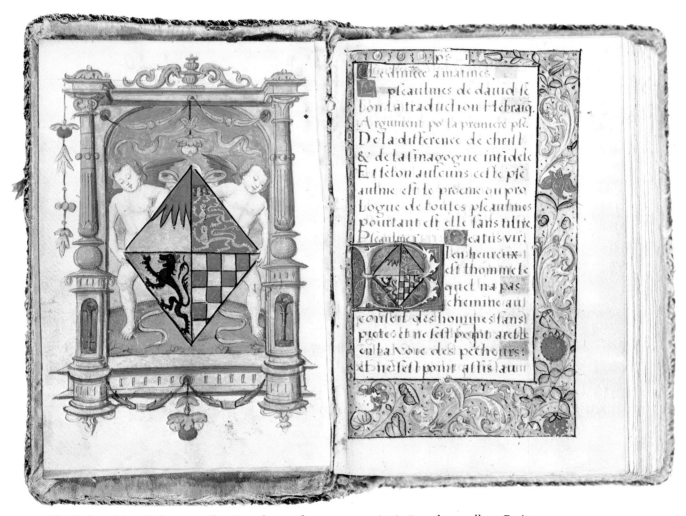

The Psalter of Anne Boleyn, two illuminated pages from a manuscript in French on vellum, Paris or Rouen, 1529–32, with an early seventeenth-century embroidered binding
London £154,000 ($246,400). 7.XII.82

This is the only surviving manuscript certainly made for Anne Boleyn and dates from the most crucial period of her life, when Henry VIII had declared his intention of making her queen and was attempting to divorce Katherine of Aragon. The book was written in France between 1529 and 1532 and its text has a double importance. It is an exceptionally early French evangelical translation from the Hebrew and is, almost certainly, the first Protestant translation of the Bible to reach the English court. Anne Boleyn had declared herself a Lutheran in the winter of 1528 and through her influence, Henry was to break with the Roman Church.

The Vision of Zechariah, one of a pair of miniatures from a Byzantine manuscript of the *Major and Minor Prophets*, on vellum, Sicily, late thirteenth century. £93,500 ($149,600)

There is no other recorded illustration to the Book of Zechariah in Byzantine art.

Acts of Mercy, four *grisaille* miniatures from an illuminated manuscript on vellum, ascribed to Simon Marmion or his immediate circle, South Flanders, *circa* 1470–80. £33,000 ($52,800)

These tiny miniatures appear to be by the same hand as those in a Book of Hours in the Bibliotheca Nazional, Madrid, ascribed by Professor Otto Pächt to Simon Marmion (*circa* 1425–89), panel painter and illuminator. They may have illustrated an elaborate Office of the Dead in a Book of Hours, or a treatise on the art of dying.

The miniatures illustrated on this page and the subjects of the following article are from an album of approximately 475 medieval illuminated cuttings, compiled in France after the French Revolution for Daniel Burckhardt-Wildt of Basel (1759–1819). They were sold in London on 25 April 1983.

The Burckhardt-Wildt Apocalypse

Nigel Morgan

The appearance of an almost completely unknown Apocalypse of *circa* 1280 was an unexpected and exciting event for the history of thirteenth-century manuscript painting. That it should survive not as a complete book but only as a series of cuttings in an album compiled for the collector Daniel Burckhardt-Wildt (1759–1819), in no way diminishes its importance. Although the text has almost all been cut away, the series of pictures is nearly complete and in excellent condition. The illustrations to the Apocalypse are preceded by a unique 'Ars Moriendi' sequence and two full-page symbolic miniatures of Trees of the Virtues and Vices. The Ars Moriendi pictures show the death and salvation of a woman (Fig. 1), which implies an intended female ownership for the Apocalypse.

Illustrated Apocalypses with half-page rectangular pictures, either in tinted drawing or full painting, set above passages of text originate in England in the 1240s. Twelve examples are known from the period up to 1280 and several more from the fourteenth century. Around 1300, copies of these English versions began to be made in France. The French copies, although stylistically largely independent of their models, follow closely the iconographic compositions of the scenes that evolved with many variations in England in the period *circa* 1240–80.

The newly discovered leaves present several problems of interpretation. They relate to a fragmentary Apocalypse of four leaves in the British Library,[1] which has almost identical iconography (Figs 2–3). Stylistically these leaves represent a later development of the same artist, with more relaxed figure forms, softer line effects in drapery and a rather different palette. The features of figure style suggest a date after 1290. Later still, the artist works on the historiated initials of an Augustinian Missal, dated on liturgical evidence after 1297.[2] The closest work in date to the cuttings, but a slightly later version of the artist's style, is an Apocalypse of *circa* 1280–90 in the Biblioteca Laurenziana in Florence (Fig. 4).[3] The Florence Apocalypse is of different format with full-page vertically orientated miniatures. Allowing for adaptations to suit this shape of frame, the iconography is very close to the cuttings (Fig. 5).

Neither the British Library fragment, nor the Florence Apocalypse, has any information to suggest place of origin or exact date. The Augustinian Missal in Baltimore gives a date after 1297 for the final phase of the style and has liturgical features of the Lorraine region. This phase of the style is continued, perhaps by a different artist, in an early fourteenth-century Apocalypse in Dresden.[4] This book has a French text in Lorraine dialect, which probably suggests it was made in or intended for that region.

Fig. 1
One of three full-page miniatures showing the death and salvation of a sinful woman,
from an Apocalypse, on vellum, possibly York or Lincoln, *circa* 1280
London £49,500 ($79,200). 25.IV.83

These miniatures were part of a group of five full-page and thirty-six half-page
double-sided miniatures, cut from an Apocalypse manuscript and mounted in an album for
Daniel Burckhardt-Wildt of Basel. In total they fetched £556,380 ($890,208).

Fig. 2   The Lamb Opens the Book, the *verso* of a cutting from the Burckhardt-Wildt
Apocalypse, with the Lamb on the *recto*
London £7,700 ($12,320). 25.IV.83

Fig. 3   The Lamb Opens the Book, from an Apocalypse
Reproduced courtesy of the British Library, London
(MS Add. 22493, fol.2 *recto*)

Fig. 4 The People Rejoicing over the Dead Witnesses Lying in the Street, from an Apocalypse
Reproduced courtesy of the Biblioteca Laurenziana, Florence (MS Ashburnham 415, fol.59 *recto*)

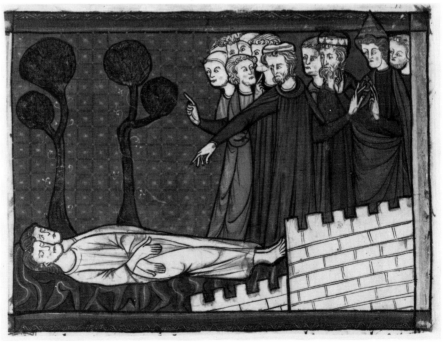

Fig. 5 The People Rejoicing over the Dead Witnesses Lying in the Street, the *verso* of a cutting from the Burckhardt-Wildt Apocalypse, with Locusts Waging War on the *recto*
London £4,620 ($7,392). 25.IV.83

Fig. 6 The Presentation in the Temple, from the
Blackburn Psalter
Reproduced courtesy of Blackburn Museum
and Art Gallery (MS Hart 21001, fol.2 *recto*)

Fig. 7 The Betrayal of Christ, from the
Blackburn Psalter
Reproduced courtesy of Blackburn Museum
and Art Gallery (MS Hart 21001, fol.3 *verso*)

In spite of these later French connections, the stylistic origins of the cuttings are in English work of the decade 1270–80. The last third of the thirteenth century is a period of strong French influence on English painting, and sometimes artists of both nationalities work together on a single manuscript or in a workshop. The workshop grouped around the 'Bible of William of Devon', named after its scribe, beginning about 1260, is a good example of such collaboration, although most of its artists are Englishmen working in a very French style whose Parisian sources have been traced. A late manuscript from this workshop, of *circa* 1270–80, is a Psalter with full-page miniatures in Blackburn Museum and Art Gallery.[5] The style is characterized by stolid figures in rigid block-like poses, rather elongated, with flat application of paint and the fold lines drawn in black (Figs 6–7). The predominant colours are a madder-red, pink, orange, a deep blue, a blue-grey and a bright green. The palette is very close to that of the cuttings, with only an ochre shadowed in olive green and an extensive use of gold grounds distinguishing the Psalter. The facial type is loosely drawn with sketchy treatment of the hair. It is very likely that the artist of the Apocalypse derived his rigid figure forms and facial types from such a style (Figs 8–9).

Another artist deriving from the Blackburn Psalter style and using a similar palette is the illuminator of the Westminster Abbey Bestiary.[6] His work, less refined than the Apocalypse painter's, has harder delineation of facial features and squatter more rigid figures, but though the source of their styles may be the same, the two artists are

Fig. 8 St John Weeping, the *verso* of a cutting from the Burckhardt-Wildt
Apocalypse, with the Worship of the Elders on the *recto*
London £10,450 ($16,720). 25.IV.83

Fig. 9 The Final Battle against Satan, the *recto* of a cutting from the
Burckhardt-Wildt Apocalypse, with the Dragon and the Beast cast into Hell on
the *verso*
London £41,800 ($66,880). 25.IV.83.

Fig. 10 The Whale, from a Bestiary
Reproduced courtesy of Gonville and Caius
College, Cambridge (MS 384/604, fol.189 *recto*)

quite distinct. The Westminster Bestiary belonged to the Franciscans of York and is related to a large group of manuscripts that can be associated with York.

Another Bestiary, in Gonville and Caius College, Cambridge,[7] comes closer to the style of the cuttings, particularly in the facial type with loosely drawn hair, doleful expressions and delicate pink touches on the cheeks (Figs 10–11). The figure style with relaxed poses and softer fold lines suggests a date *circa* 1290. This Bestiary belonged in the late Middle Ages to the vicar of Dowsby in north Lincolnshire. The Blackburn Psalter has a calendar for the diocese of Lincoln, with which region other 'Bible of William of Devon' group manuscripts have connections. These fragmentary pieces of evidence for the related manuscripts point to some link with the diocese of Lincoln or York for these stylistic developments. Christopher de Hamel in the sale catalogue has suggested a possible York origin for the Apocalypse cuttings, making some interesting parallels with the stained glass of the chapter house.

This must be set against the later links with Lorraine, mentioned above. Artists travelling to work between France and England were common at the time and this might provide an explanation. Perhaps the illuminator of the cuttings began his career in the York/Lincoln region around 1280 and then travelled around 1290 to France, eventually becoming established in Lorraine. Alternatively the artist may have been a Frenchman who formed his early style from an English Apocalypse of the 'William of Devon' group. Further research may help to clarify these hypotheses.

The iconography of the Apocalypse illustrations also provides interesting problems. No extant English or French Apocalypse known to me has exactly the same sequence of subjects as the cuttings and their companion set in the Florence manuscript. The basic series of pictures is closely dependent on the Lambeth Palace Apocalypse of *circa* 1260,[8] but several scenes are quite different (eg Figs 4–5), and several scenes

Fig. 11 The Dragon Waging War, the *recto* of a cutting from the Burckhardt-Wildt Apocalypse, with the Beast of the Sea on the *verso*
London £14,300 ($22,880). 25.IV.83
Now in the Detroit Institute of Arts (Gift of the Founder's Junior Council and Mr and Mrs Walter Buhl Ford II Fund)

combined into one frame in Lambeth are separated as individual miniatures in the Burckhardt-Wildt Apocalypse. The interpretative treatment of the Lambeth cycle suggests either derivation from a lost intermediary, or that the artist of this manuscript was the originator of the new subjects. In view of the stylistic origins in work like the Blackburn Psalter, it is a reasonable hypothesis that a lost intermediary existed in that style. No Apocalypse has come down to us from the 'Bible of William of Devon' group, but perhaps such a book is the missing link. The model must have been fully painted, not in tinted drawing as are many English Apocalypses, with an idiosyncratic preference for blue hair for the older men. This feature is prominent in the cuttings (Figs 8–9), and is continued as late as the Baltimore Missal and the Dresden Apocalypse. Blue hair is first extensively used in the Trinity College Apocalypse of *circa* 1250–60, from which this oddity must ultimately be derived.[9]

These theories on the date and origin of the new discovery must necessarily be preliminary to a more detailed investigation. The appearance of an unpublished Apocalypse has produced more problems for art historians than it has provided solutions. Whatever the eventual explanations, these fine cuttings add considerably to our understanding of a complex period of English painting.

I am most grateful to Alison Stones for pointing out some of the French parallels and for discussion of the problems of the leaves, on several points of which we hold differing interpretations.

NOTES

1. MS Add. 22493
2. Walters Art Gallery, Baltimore, MS W. 127
3. MS Ashburnham 415
4. Sächsische Landesbibliothek, MS Oc. 50
5. MS Hart 21001
6. Westminster Abbey Library, MS 22
7. MS 384/604
8. MS 209
9. MS R. 16.2

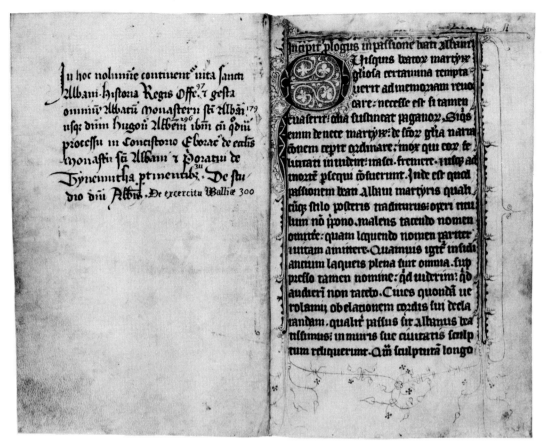

Life of St Alban and other historical texts, two pages from a manuscript on vellum, St Albans Abbey,
early fourteenth century
London £55,000 ($88,000). 13.VI.83
From the collection of the Most Hon. the Marquess of Bute

This volume was copied for the personal use of the Abbot of St Albans, probably Hugh de Eversdone
(1308–26). It contains five texts relating to the abbey's history and endowment, including two
compiled by Matthew Paris (d. 1259), monk of St Albans, the celebrated thirteenth-century historian
and illuminator. The most important of them, his *Lives of the Abbots of St Albans*, is one of the finest
thirteenth-century historical texts and gives a uniquely detailed insight into the library and
intellectual life of one of the great English monastic centres of learning.

Opposite
As Henry VI is portrayed as a saint and there is an emphasis on the feasts
of Edward the Confessor and St George, this manuscript may have been
illuminated for a nobleman of the royal household. The manuscript is
remarkable for its size, the extent of its decoration and its extraordinarily fresh
condition. It was bought by the 4th Marquess of Bute for £1,100 in about 1915,
when it was described as made for Henry VIII.

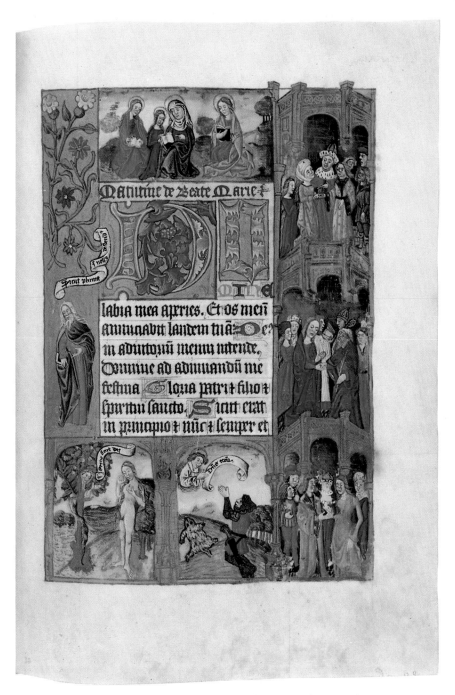

Book of Hours, the opening of Matins with an illuminated border of St Anne
teaching the Virgin to read, three marriages, Gideon and the fleece, and the
Temptation of Eve, from a manuscript partly in Middle English, with fifty-three
large miniatures and many illuminated borders, on vellum, possibly London or
Windsor, *circa* 1500–20
London £154,000 ($246,400). 13.VI.83
From the collection of the Most Hon. the Marquess of Bute

Psalms, biblical hymns and other texts, Virgin and Child, one of thirty-seven miniatures from a
manuscript in Ethiopic, on vellum, fifteenth century
London £37,400 ($59,840). 20.VI.83
From the collection of the Hagop Kevorkian Fund

Fighting water buffaloes, a Mughal drawing, attributed to Farrukh Chela, late sixteenth century, $6\frac{7}{8}$in by $9\frac{1}{2}$in (17.6cm by 24cm)
London £82,500 ($132,000). 20.VI.83
From the Pan–Asian Collection formed by the late Christian Humann

RASHID AL-DIN
A Survey and Index of Rashid al-Din's Works, a page from a Persian manuscript in *naskh* script,
scriptorium of Rashid al-Din, Tabriz, dated 1307, 1316 and 1317
London £37,400 ($59,840). 18.IV.83
From the collection of the Hagop Kevorkian Fund

Rashid al-Din, distinguished physician, vizier and historian, encouraged the copying of his works,
but few have survived as the scriptorium was plundered after his execution in 1318. A fragment of
his richly illustrated *World History* was sold at Sotheby's on 8 July 1980.

וְנִלְחַם בָּנוּ וְעָלָה מִן הָאָרֶץ וַיְעַנּוּנוּ כְּמָה שֶׁנֶּאֱמַר וַיָּשִׂימוּ

עָלָיו שָׂרֵי מִסִּים לְמַעַן עַנֹּתוֹ בְּסִבְלֹתָם וַיִּבֶן עָרֵי מִסְכְּנוֹת

לְפַרְעֹה אֶת פִּתֹם וְאֶת רַעַמְסֵס : וַיִּתְּנוּ עָלֵינוּ עֲבֹדָה קָשָׁה

כְּמָה שֶׁנֶּאֱמַר וַיַּעֲבִדוּ מִצְרַיִם אֶת בְּנֵי יִשְׂרָאֵל בְּפָרֶךְ : וַנִּצְעַק

אֶל יְיָ אֱלֹהֵי אֲבֹתֵינוּ וַיִּשְׁמַע יְיָ אֶת קֹלֵנוּ וַיַּרְא אֶת עָנְיֵנוּ וְאֶת עֲמָלֵנוּ

וְאֶת לַחֲצֵנוּ : וַנִּצְעַק אֶל יְיָ אֱלֹהֵי אֲבֹתֵינוּ כְּמָה שֶׁנֶּאֱמַר וַיְהִי בַיָּמִים

הָרַבִּים הָהֵם וַיָּמָת מֶלֶךְ מִצְרַיִם וַיֵּאָנְחוּ בְנֵי יִשְׂרָאֵל מִן הָעֲבֹדָה

The Leipnik Haggadah, the building of Pithom and Ra'amses, one of sixty-two miniatures from a manuscript in Hebrew, Old Yiddish and Ladino, in Ashkenazi and cursive Hebrew script, on vellum, illuminated by Joseph Leipnik, Altona, 1736–37
New York $264,000 (£165,000). 23.VI.83

Joseph Leipnik was the most important and innovative Jewish illuminator in eighteenth-century Germany. He broke away from the stylized illustrations of contemporary printed *haggadot* and drew on his knowledge of the Old Masters to paint vividly coloured miniatures.

Stravinsky's *Le sacre du printemps*

Louis Cyr

There can be no doubt that the first performance of Stravinsky's *Le sacre du printemps*, regarded as the composer's most controversial and innovative work, shattered the complacency of the European musical establishment at its première in Paris on 29 May 1913. The appearance of the autograph manuscript containing the first full-scale draft of the work at Sotheby's was an event of great importance (Fig. 1). This draft, which realized the highest price ever paid for a music manuscript, contains much new information about the origins of the work and is a 'missing link' between the two important sources already known to scholars, in the Collection Meyer, Paris, and in the Sacher Collection, Basel, where this draft now joins the autograph full score.

Before embarking, in the mid-1920s, on an international career as a concert pianist and conductor as well as a composer, Stravinsky was at times frustratingly dependent on the financial support of close friends and benefactors. During the war years, 1914–18, which he lived out with his young family in Swiss exile, Stravinsky saw former lucrative financial ties with his native Russia gradually severed. Nor did the Ballets Russes and Diaghilev fare much better. The unpleasant quarrels between the latter and Stravinsky in 1919–20, concerning author's rights and performance fees to be paid to the composer for *L'oiseau de feu*, *Petrouchka* and the commission of *Les noces*, are a tragic witness to the sorry financial plight Stravinsky experienced along with most musicians and dancers during the immediate post-war years in Europe.

Many friends and benefactors did, however, come to the rescue, either with monetary contributions, or by commissioning a work from the composer. Some wished to remain anonymous, other patrons were well known, including Lord Berners, Princesse Edmond de Polignac, Vicomtesse Marie-Laure de Noailles, Werner Reinhart, Misia Sert and Gabrielle 'Coco' Chanel. Stravinsky's usual token of appreciation was the gift of sketches for a work, a complete manuscript, parts thereof, or an annotated printed score. Thus, for example, Werner Reinhart was rewarded in June 1923 with a beautifully bound copy of a variety of sketches for *Les noces*. The day after the première of *Le sacre du printemps*, Misia Sert was given an extensively annotated four-hand piano version that Stravinsky had used in helping Nijinsky compose the work's first choreography. A reconciled Diaghilev earned a bound collection of sketches for *Le sacre* in 1921 and, arriving at the manuscript involved in last November's historic sale, Coco Chanel was rewarded with the first draft score. She had financially underwritten the December 1920 revival of *Le sacre* in Paris, and her intimate relationship with the composer at the time was hardly a secret. Although their mutual feelings had cooled considerably by the late 1920s, Chanel nevertheless

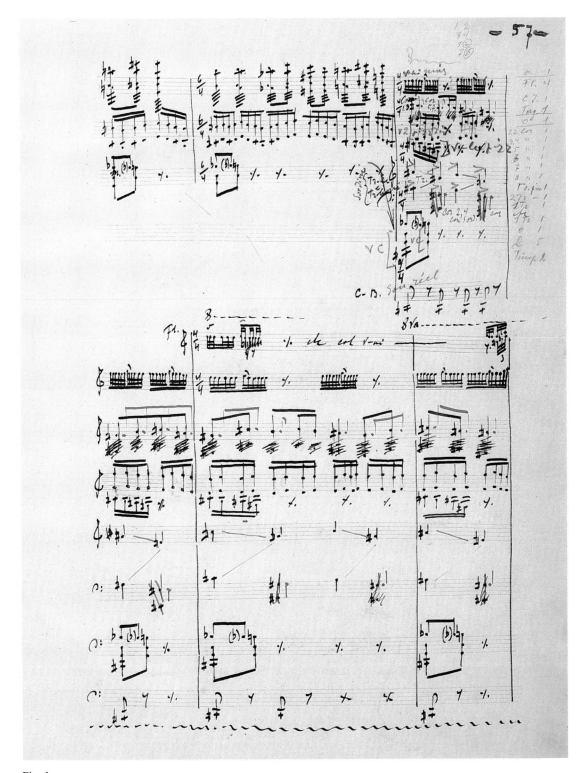

Fig. 1

IGOR STRAVINSKY

An autograph working draft of *Le sacre du printemps*, omitting only the final section, the *Danse sacrale*, sixty-seven pages, signed and dated on the third flyleaf *I. Strawinski 1911–12–13 Mart* and the introduction to the second part *Igor Strawinsky Clarens 19/III 1913*

London £330,000 ($528,000). 11.XI.82

Now in the collection of the Sacher Foundation, Basel

hung on to the precious manuscript, allowing it to be seen in the 'Ballets Russes de Diaghilev' exhibition in Paris in 1939, at the Musée des Arts Décoratifs. The manuscript was later in the possession of the famous Russian–French dancer and choreographer Serge Lifar, whose signature is found on the title page.

With its acquisition for the Sacher Foundation, a vital and most significant link in the creative stages of this epoch-making ballet score has surfaced for good. Scholars will soon be able to compare it at leisure with the complete manuscript autograph full score already belonging to the Foundation and with the published sketches (page references below refer to this collection, published in 1969 by Boosey & Hawkes).

Even a fleeting examination of the manuscript is enough to whet one's appetite. Its most obvious characteristic is that it is missing the *Danse sacrale*. Such an omission can be best explained if the *Danse* had been drafted separately and was still in Nijinsky's possession at the time of Stravinsky's donation to Chanel. Its present whereabouts remain unknown.

The last twenty pages in Stravinsky's workbook are largely blank, but not completely. On pages numbered 65 (Fig. 2) to 67 one unexpectedly finds a detailed, heavily corrected, but complete draft of the present beginning of the introduction to part two, dated *19/III 13* and covering rehearsal numbers 79 to 85. These three pages are to be inserted 'before p.37' of the manuscript, where one discovers that the introduction to part two originally began with the trumpet duo at rehearsal number 86, without the least hint of further expansion. This is confirmed, first by the initial sketches (pp.50–65, especially p.63), which only contain the ingredients for the original introduction to part two, and also by the autograph full score, where the new beginning to this introduction was inserted later on extra pages and dated 29 March 1913. Previously undated sketches for this new beginning (pp.104–107) can probably now be dated precisely between 9 and 15 March 1913. Thus the new addition to the introduction to part two was the last major compositional problem Stravinsky had to resolve on finishing the full score, dated 8 March 1913, even as Pierre Monteux was beginning rehearsals for part one of *Le sacre*. At this late stage, sketches, first draft and full score follow closely upon one another.

In a similar way it would seem that, a year earlier, only five days separate the first draft score of the end of part one (*Danse de la terre*), dated 24 February 1912, and its full orchestral score, completed on 29 February 1912. Stravinsky was hurrying to meet the then projected deadline of a première in May 1912.

Most often, however, this manuscript leans towards the early sketches of *Le sacre*, remaining remote from the autograph full score. So further detailed sketches, and possibly drafts, must still be sought to fit in between the final instrumentation and the short-score manuscript. One has only to compare an excerpt from the *Glorification de l'élue* with the present rehearsal numbers 118–19, to measure the innumerable transformations still to come. In at least two instances the manuscript seems to antedate even the available sketches: for example, bars 3–5 of the beginning of the present *Jeu du rapt* are missing completely, although two detailed and complete sketches of the passage have survived (p.126).

Among the many instrumental differences worthy of note are the missing celli 'pizzicati' in the introduction to part one (rehearsal numbers 7, 10–11). Equally, the

Fig. 2
The new beginning to the introduction
to the second part, on p. 65 of the
draft score

second violins' lengthy 'col legno' in the *Augures printaniers* was originally 'pizzicato' throughout. As in the sketches, percussion instruments are still conspicuously absent in many sections, as are most dynamics. And the majority of metronomic indications are, in both sketches and first draft, faster than those eventually adopted.

Most perplexing of all, however, is the inconsistent layout of the draft score. Without any apparent logic, lengthy two-hand passages lacking any instrumental, tempo or dynamic indications, which appear occasionally even in the sketches, alternate with detailed orchestrated passages that represent substantial steps away from the sketches. Some of the two-stave sections could even have been extracted and transferred to the published four-hand version with only minor modifications.

The most important, albeit tentative, conclusion seems to be that there are very complex connections between this short-score draft, earlier sketches, later sketches and drafts, and the autograph full score. It does not represent a simple transition between sketches and full score:

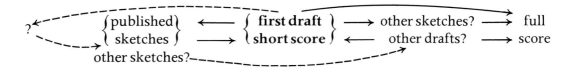

Thus musicologists specializing in Stravinsky's work habits now have an even more fascinating task carved out for them.

Vocabularius Teutonicus–Latinus, with the hedgehog bookplate of Johannes Knabensberg, *circa* 1485
London £8,250 ($13,200). 27.V.83

Johannes Knabensberg was chaplain to the Bavarian family of Schoenstett; the hedgehog (*Igel*) is a pun on his nickname, 'Igler'. This is one of the three earliest surviving bookplate designs.

Opposite
JOHANN SEBASTIAN BACH
An autograph manuscript of the cantata *O Ewigkeit, du Donnerwort,* BWV 20, twenty-one pages, Leipzig, before 11 June 1724
London £209,000 ($334,400). 11.XI.82

This manuscript is the fullest source for the work, which inaugurated Bach's second cycle of church cantatas. It vividly illustrates the composer's working practice in the amount of corrected material, and his efforts to economize on paper can be seen in the crowded staves.

LUDWIG VAN BEETHOVEN
Four pages from an autograph sketchbook, containing early versions of five major works, including the Piano Concerto no. 1 in C major, 1800
London £27,500 ($44,000). 26.V.83

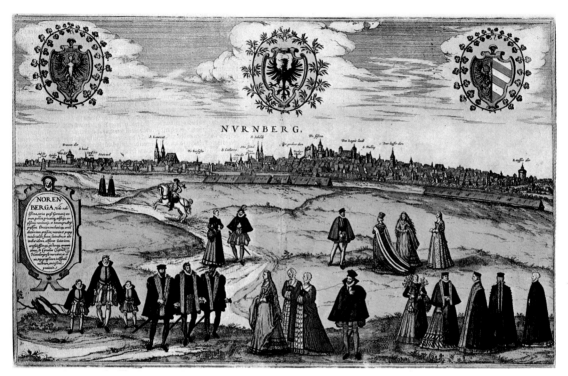

GEORG BRAUN and FRANZ HOGENBERG
Civitates Orbis Terrarum, five volumes, with 303 hand-coloured engraved plates,
Cologne, 1582–1600?
London £37,950 ($60,720). 25.XI.82

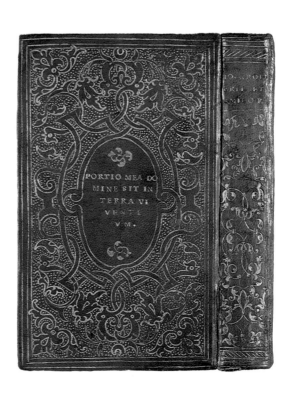

CORNELIUS SCHEPPER
*Rerum à Carolo . V . Caesare Augusto in Africa
bello gestarum commentarij*, with three
double-page woodcut maps and plans, bound for
Jean Grolier in red morocco with gilt tooling by
the Cupid's Bow Binder, Antwerp, 1554
London £13,200 ($21,120). 27.V.83

TANYSIPTERA NIGRICEPS, Sclater.

JOHN GOULD
The Birds of New Guinea and the adjacent Papuan Islands, five volumes, 320 hand-coloured
lithographed plates by John Gould and W. Hart, 1875–88
London £13,750 ($22,000). 29.XI.82

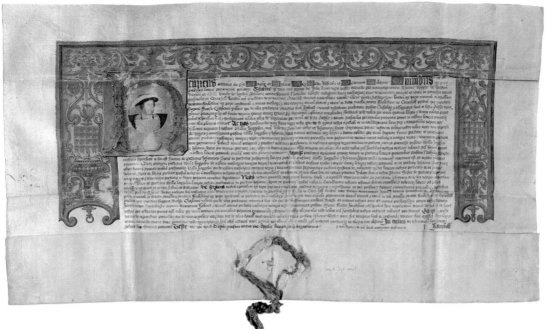

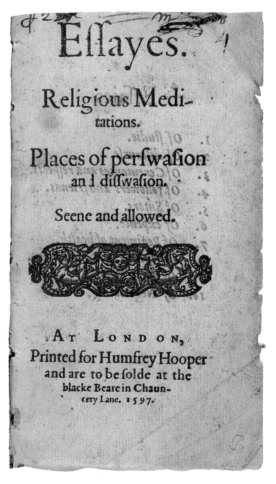

Above

HENRY VIII

A Royal Letters Patent with an illuminated initial-letter portrait of
Henry VIII by Lucas Hornebolte, on vellum, with the Great Seal of
Henry VIII, Westminster, 28 April 1524
London £9,680 ($15,488). 11.VII.83

Lucas Hornebolte begins the English tradition of limning, or
miniature painting, and appears to have taught Holbein the
technique. The painting on this newly discovered Royal Letters
Patent is Hornebolte's earliest datable work and is unusual in
that initial-letter portraits on documents were generally
executed by scribes rather than limners.

Right

FRANCIS BACON

Essayes, second edition, 1597, bound with *The Wisedome of
the Ancients*, 1619
London £20,900 ($33,440). 21.VII.83

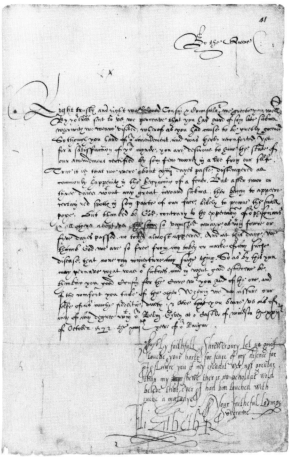

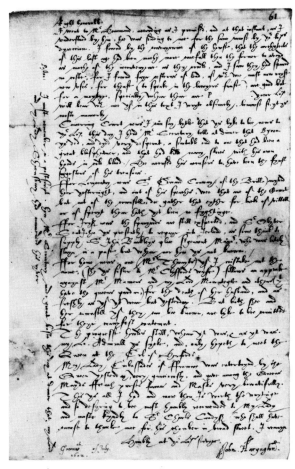

ELIZABETH I
A letter to George Talbot, 6th Earl of Shrewsbury, signed with an autograph postscript commenting on her recent attack of smallpox, 22 October 1572

SIR JOHN HARINGTON
An autograph letter to Gilbert Talbot, 7th Earl of Shrewsbury, discussing the use of some 'fayr cesterns of lead', Greenwich, July 1602

The private treaty sale of the Talbot papers to Lambeth Palace Library, London, was negotiated by Sotheby's.

The Talbot papers, preserved since the late seventeenth century in the College of Arms, constitute one of the most important Tudor archives. Comprising over 2,500 letters and documents of the Talbot family, Earls of Shrewsbury, written between 1499 and 1611, they provide a detailed record of one of the most influential families of the age. Many famous names of the period are represented: they range from Elizabeth I, who comments on an attack of smallpox which has left her unscathed (see above, left) and expresses her indebtedness to the 6th Earl for his sixteen-year guardianship of Mary Queen of Scots, to the notorious persecutor of recusants, Richard Topcliffe, who writes about the rooting out of 'daindgeroos & loathesomest treasons'. There are letters on the beheading 'this day' of Lady Jane Grey, the 'tragecall newes' of the Massacre of St Bartholomew and the queen's review of the troops at Tilbury before the Spanish Armada. Among the literary figures represented are Robert Sidney, reporting news of a masque being written by Ben Jonson, and the poet Sir John Harington, inventor of the water closet, who writes of some 'fayr cesterns of lead' that he is putting to obscure use (see above, right). Documents of major importance to historians of drama include a Privy Council letter of 1556 banning all plays and players from the realm and Robert Dudley's application for the licensing of his troupe of players three years later. Incessant border fighting between the English and the Scots is often described, including events leading up to the Battle of Pinkie (10 September 1547). The urgency of the times finds expression in courier instructions on innumerable letters, 'Haste, post haste, for thy life, for thy life'.

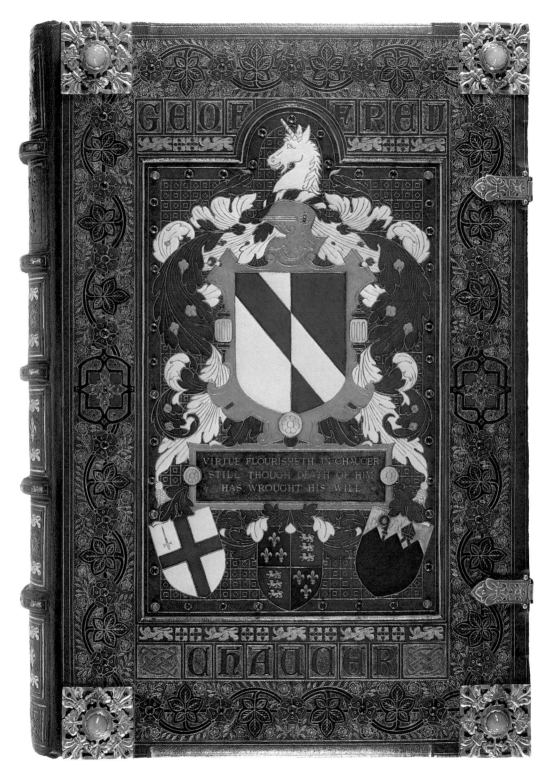

GEOFFREY CHAUCER
Works, with eighty-seven woodcuts after Sir Edward Coley Burne-Jones and decorations after
William Morris, bound in inlaid and jewelled brown morocco by Sangorski and Sutcliffe,
Kelmscott Press, 1896
London £21,450 ($34,320). 24.V.83

FAISAL I OF IRAQ
An autograph diary in Arabic kept during the Paris
Peace Conference of 1919, containing his proposals for
the setting up of independent Arab states,
about 100 pages, December 1918–April 1919
London £121,000 ($193,600). 28.III.83

This diary ranges over the events leading up to and
including the conference, which was to prove
disastrous for Faisal's own future and that of the Arab
nations. T. E. Lawrence had suggested that Faisal
should represent his father in Paris and acted as his
interpreter during the sessions. In the text, Faisal pays
warm tribute to Lawrence and reveals his own
reactions to this important event in the recent history
of the Middle East.

MARCEL PROUST
A group of seventeen autograph letters to his
mother and eight of her letters to him,
seventy-six pages,
17 October 1902–August 1905
London £29,700 ($47,520). 26.V.83

Many of the incidents recounted in these
letters reappear in A la Recherche du Temps
Perdu (1913–28).

GEORGE WASHINGTON
An autograph letter to Richard Henry Lee, concerning
the progress of the American War of Independence,
two pages, Valley Forge, 25 May 1778
New York $60,500 (£37,813). 26.IV.83

THE TREATY OF PARIS
A group of eighteen manuscripts and printed
documents relating to negotiations to end the American
Revolution, dating from the 1776 commission of
Lord Richard and General William Howe to the final
Treaty of Paris, 3 September 1783, its ratification
and implementation
New York $110,000 (£68,750). 26.IV.83

SIEGFRIED SASSOON
The autograph manuscripts, typescripts and corrected proofs for *Memoirs of an Infantry Officer*, nine volumes, 1917–30
New York $35,750 (£22,344). 15.X.82

Below, left and right
WILLIAM HENRY HARRISON
An autograph letter to R. Buchanan on personal business affairs, two pages, Washington DC, 10 March 1841
New York $132,000 (£82,500). 26.IV.83

This is a rare autograph letter from the period of Harrison's brief presidency of the United States.

Coins and medals

Right
The Most Noble Order of the Garter (KG), Lesser George
(sash badge), gold and enamel, *circa* 1820
London £8,000 ($12,800). 21.X.82

Below
The Imperial Order of the Crown of India (CI), awarded to
Florence, Countess of Kimberley in 1883
London £6,500 ($10,400). 3.III.83

UMAYYAD, dinar of Yazid II, AH 103 (721 AD),
Ifriqiya mint
£24,000 ($38,400)

AYYUBID, dinar of Saladin, AH 583 (1187 AD), Dimashq
(Damascus) mint
£26,000 ($41,600)

This coin was probably struck to mark the defeat of the
crusader kingdom in the Holy Land at the Battle of Hattin
in 1187, and the reconquest of Jerusalem the same year.

DELHI SULTANATE, dinar of Shams al-din Iltutmush,
AH 614 (1217 AD)
£5,500 ($8,800)

FATIMID, dinar struck by the Shiite partisan
al-Basasiri, AH 451 (1059 AD), Madinat al-Salam
(Baghdad) mint
£15,000 ($24,000)

ABBASID, dinar of al-Muqtadi, AH 486 (1093 AD),
Madinat al-Salam (Baghdad) mint
£8,500 ($13,600)

The Islamic gold coins on this page were sold in London on 20 April 1983.
They are illustrated one and a half times actual size.

Left
ANCIENT GREEK, Thrace, tetradrachm of Mesembria, *circa* 400 BC
SFr 55,000 (£16,418:$26,269)

Right
ANCIENT GREEK, Phokis, stater of Delphi, struck by the Amphiktyonic Council (336–334 BC)
SFr 60,500 (£18,060:$28,896)

ANCIENT GREECE, Egyptian dekadrachm of Berenike II, wife of Ptolemy III (246–221 BC)
SFr 41,800 (£12,478:$19,965)

JEWISH, half shekel of year 4 of the Jewish Revolt against the Romans (66–70 AD)
SFr 121,000 (£36,119:$57,790)

JEWISH, shekel of year 5 of the Jewish Revolt against the Romans (66–70 AD)
SFr 352,000 (£105,075:$168,120)

ROMAN, 4 aurei medallion of Maximian Hercules, 303 AD, Trier mint
SFr 143,000 (£42,687:$68,299)
This coin is from the important hoard found near Arras, France, in 1922, and was struck to commemorate the vicennalia of Diocletian and Maximian towards the end of 303 AD.

Left
ROMAN, aureus of Septimius Severus and Caracalla, 204 AD
SFr 50,600 (£15,104:$24,166)

Right
ROMAN, aureus of Severus II as Caesar (305–306 AD), Ticinum mint
SFr 39,600 (£11,821:$18,914)

The Greek and Roman silver and gold coins illustrated on this page are from the Virgil M. Brand Collection and were sold in Zurich on 9 June 1983.

Left
CHUR, 7 ducats of Bishop Johann V
Flugi von Aspermont, 1615
SFr 49,500 (£14,776:$23,642)

Right
BASEL, 5 ducats, or *Gluckhennenthaler*
struck in gold, seventeenth century
SFr 22,000 (£6,567:$10,507)

LAUSANNE, ducat of Bishop Aymon
von Montfaucon (1491–1517)
SFr 19,800 (£5,910:$9,456)

SCHWYZ, ducat depicting St Martin,
1653
SFr 22,000 (£6,567:$10,507)

Right
OBWALDEN, 5 ducats, or half thaler
struck in gold, 1732
SFr 41,800 (£12,478:$19,965)

Left and right
LUCERNE, medallic 14 ducats, or thaler
struck in gold, 1699
SFr 44,000 (£13,134:$21,014)

The Swiss gold coins illustrated on this page are from the Virgil M. Brand Collection and were sold in
Zurich on 11 November 1982.

The S. Hallock du Pont and Scott-Kinnear Collections of American gold coins

Michael Hodder

During the 1982–83 season two remarkable, specialized collections of coins were dispersed through Sotheby's New York auction rooms. The S. Hallock du Pont Collection contained one of the most complete collections of United States gold dollars, Quarter Eagles (gold $2.50 pieces), Half Eagles (gold $5 pieces) and Eagles (gold $10 pieces) to come to auction in many years, as well as a complete set of the extremely rare Stellas (gold $4 pieces). The Scott-Kinnear Collection had been built around the pioneer coins of the early American settlements in northern California and the later issues of the subsidiary mint established in San Francisco in 1854. Both collections offered a rare and informative glimpse of the history of coinage in the United States, illustrated by many early, elusive and extremely rare coins that are lacking in most collections.

During the American War of Independence, the Continental Congress authorized the issue of currency notes and paper money, and the individual states of the Confederation also issued currency notes, but no coinage was struck by the embattled young nation. Although an official U.S. Mint was authorized by Congress in 1782, one year before the Treaty of Paris, ten years were to elapse before the government issued coins struck in its own minting facilities. During these years, Congress acquiesced in the circulation of coins struck by private coiners in Great Britain for the American market, also accepting Spanish milled dollars as lawful payment for public debts.

The first U.S. Mint was authorized by another Act of Congress in 1792 to be staffed by the necessary artists and coiners. The act set the types of coins to be struck, with their metallic contents and finenesses, from copper half cents to gold Eagles. Three more years passed before the first issue of gold coins was actually made, a small number of $5 and $10 pieces. Quarter Eagles were first produced the following year, 1796 (Fig. 1). These early coins were struck on screw presses, using dies engraved by hand. The engraving is usually very good, but the striking pressures, applied by the hand-operated presses to transfer the design from the dies to the coin blanks, varied from the adequate to the plainly inadequate (Figs 2–3). Consequently, each piece is readily identifiable by collectors, because each is slightly different.

This first mint, in Philadelphia, operated until the introduction of more sophisticated steam presses in the 1830s. Apart from technological problems, which naturally limited the number of coins that could be produced, the early mint faced a severe shortage of bullion. After 1799, United States coins in both silver and gold were worth more than

Fig. 1
Left
Quarter Eagle, 1796
New York $6,050(£3,781). 21.IX.82
From the collection of the late S. Hallock du Pont

Fig. 2
Right
Quarter Eagle, 1808
New York $19,800(£12,375). 21.IX.82
From the collection of the late S. Hallock du Pont

Fig. 3
Left
Half Eagle, 1811
New York $2,530(£1,581). 21.IX.82
From the collection of the late S. Hallock du Pont

Fig. 4
Right
Above Eagle, 1907
New York $33,000(£20,625). 14.X.82
From the Scott-Kinnear Collection
Below Eagle, 1933
New York $78,100(£48,813). 4.III.83
From the collection of the late S. Hallock du Pont

Fig. 5
Left
Above Stella, 1880, flowing-hair variety
New York $44,000(£27,500). 21.IX.82
From the collection of the late S. Hallock du Pont
Below Stella, 1880, coiled-hair variety
New York $102,300(£63,938). 21.IX.82
From the collection of the late S. Hallock du Pont

their face values on the international bullion market, and consequently American coins tended to leave home circulation for European melting pots. This situation was remedied in 1834, when the weights were reduced, but the net effect of low production capacity and a shortage of bullion has made gold issues of 1795–1834 very scarce, and many are of the highest rarity today.

Until 1933 United States coins and currency were officially backed by gold, but in March of that year Congress resolved that the country's money should no longer be redeemable in specie. This act was passed during the Great Depression, when supplies of bullion were needed to liquidate the national debt and for foreign trade transactions. From 1834 to 1933, the period of standardized production methods in the mint (Fig. 4), availability of bullion for coining and the vicissitudes of American foreign trade were the two most influential factors affecting the output of the various minting facilities. During the American Civil War, when bullion was scarcer than usual, production of gold coins in the eastern mints declined to very low levels. After the country had recovered from the war, an attempt was made to manufacture a coin which would not only have currency in the United States, but would also bear on its face a value in internationally recognized units of weight and fineness. These experimental pieces, $4 gold coins known as Stellas (Fig. 5), were not finally adopted.

The first, and chief, U.S. Mint was located in Philadelphia, and for the first fifty years of American history all coins were struck there. The discovery of gold in North Carolina and Georgia led to the establishment of branch, or subsidiary, mints in Charlotte (Fig. 6) and Dahlonega in the late 1830s, where coins were struck until the capture of the towns by the Army of the Confederacy in 1861. Local bullion supplies contained trace elements which lent unusual colouring to the coins, and whereas the Philadelphia mint was using steam presses at the time, the local mints were given the older screw presses. These two factors, combined with the ever-dwindling supplies of gold bullion, make branch-mint strikes distinctive in appearance, usually poor in workmanship, but scarce and so highly collectable.

The greatest discovery of gold in American history came in 1848, when nuggets of alluvial gold were found along the Sacramento and Russian Rivers in California. As part of the territory of California's effort to gain admission to the Union as a new state, a small quantity of the newly discovered gold was shipped overland to Philadelphia for coining into Quarter Eagles. These coins were stamped CAL, to attest to the origin of the bullion, and distributed among members of Congress and the President's staff (Fig. 7). Statehood followed in 1850 and a local mint, to be erected in San Francisco, was authorized the following year, but not completed until 1854. From 1849 to 1855 the coinage needs of California were supplied by local coiners established in San Francisco and striking coins to their own designs (which often echoed national ones) from gold nuggets and dust brought from the gold fields by miners (Fig. 8). Likewise, gold discovered in Colorado was coined in Denver by a local minting firm. The most successful private coiners, Curtis & Perry of San Francisco, and Clark, Gruber & Co. of Denver (Fig. 9), bequeathed their offices and equipment to the national government when branch mints were authorized in their cities. The largest gold coin ever struck by the United States, a $50 piece, was minted in San Francisco in 1915, to commemorate the opening of the Panama Canal (Fig. 10).

Figs 6–7
Above Quarter Eagle, 1838, Charlotte mint
New York $935 (£584). 21.IX.82
From the collection of the late S. Hallock du Pont
Below Quarter Eagle, 1848 CAL
New York $16,500 (£10,313). 14.X.82
From the Scott-Kinnear Collection

Fig. 8
Above Baldwin & Co., 10 dollars, 1850, the 'Vaquero',
New York $42,900 (£26,813). 14.X.82
From the Scott-Kinnear Collection
Below Baldwin & Co., 20 dollars, 1851
New York $63,250 (£39,531). 14.X.82
From the Scott-Kinnear Collection

Fig. 9
Clark, Gruber & Co., 10 dollars, 1860, 'Pikes Peak Gold'
New York $6,050 (£3,781). 14.X.82
From the Scott-Kinnear Collection

Fig. 10
50 dollars, 1915, San Francisco mint, for
the Panama–Pacific Exposition
New York $36,300 (£22,688). 14.X.82
From the Scott-Kinnear Collection

Arms and armour

A Hispano-Moresque sallet, second half fifteenth century
London £82,500 ($132,000). 5.V.83
From the collection of the Lord Astor of Hever

According to tradition, this sallet belonged to Boabdil, last Moorish King of Granada (1481–91):
the *cloisonné* ornament is similar to that on the hilt of the sword of Boabdil in the Museo de
Artillería, Madrid. No other medieval helmet retaining such *cloisonné* decoration is known.

A German bascinet with pig-face visor, *circa* 1400
London £107,800 ($172,480). 5.V.83
From the collection of the Lord Astor of Hever

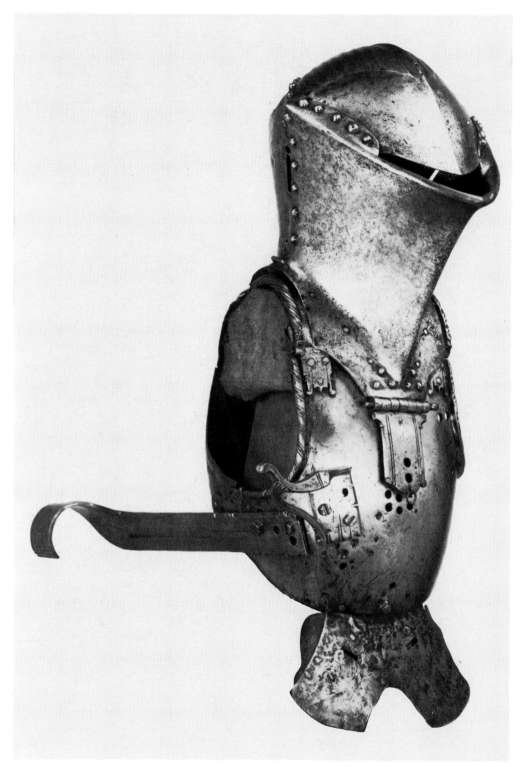

A German tilt armour, second half fifteenth century
London £187,000 ($299,200). 5.V.83
From the collection of the Lord Astor of Hever

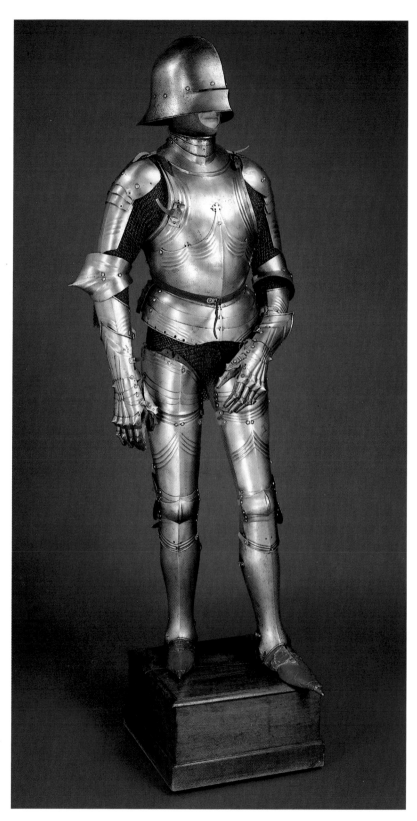

A Tirolese suit of armour, late
fifteenth century, the jambs Milanese,
second half fifteenth century
London £115,500 ($184,800). 5.V.83
From the collection of the Lord Astor
of Hever

The salade is wrought in one piece
and struck with the two marks of
Adrian Treytz of Mühlau, near
Innsbruck. The Treytz family
included no fewer than six Innsbruck
armourers over several generations.
Adrian Treytz the Elder is recorded
as *Harnischmeister* in Mühlau
in 1475, working for Archduke
Sigismund. The greaves are struck
with the mark of Alvisio da Boltego,
who worked in Milan and is known
to have been associated with the
Negroli family of armourers.

The Negroli armour from Hever Castle

Johannes Auersperg

The sale of the contents of Hever Castle brought under the hammer the finest selection of arms and armour to appear in the auction room since the war; one of the greatest collections in private hands. The sale leapt into the headlines when the most important of the fourteen suits of armour fetched a record-breaking price (Fig. 1). The dramatic bidding reflected a royal connection and an association with a famous armourer.

In the late seventeenth century, the armour was in the collection of the French minister Colbert, who had been given it by his master, Louis XIV. Colbert was a well-known collector of curiosities, works of art and antiquities and it was common for princes to give splendid presents to their favourites, often from their own collections. It seems likely that the suit came from the Royal Arsenal in Paris, as the burgonet or parade helmet, which once belonged to the same garniture, remained there. It was later transferred to the Louvre, where it can still be seen (Fig. 2).

A miniature provides proof of the armour's original owner (Fig. 3). It portrays the young Henry of Valois, King Henry II of France (1547–59), wearing the suit on horseback. Armour of this splendour was worn only a few times, and it is more than likely that Henry was wearing his latest acquisition when he was painted. His youthfulness possibly suggests that he is shown as Dauphin. This would date the armour before 1547.

Henry and his father, Francis I, were both enthusiastic patrons of armourers. The turn of the century and the following decades had seen the more important European princes competing for the best armourers and gunsmiths to work at their courts. This resulted in the foundation of some outstanding workshops, where increasingly splen-didly decorated and elaborate armours were produced; for example, at Innsbruck (for Emperor Maximilian), Milan (for the Sforza), Greenwich (for Henry VIII), and Fontainebleau and Paris (for Francis I). However, many of the best craftsmen remained free agents, employed for particular commissions, either at the royal armouries or in their own workshops.

The few surviving late Renaissance and Mannerist suits of armour fall into two groups. The first and earlier of them corresponds to the traditional fighting suit. Some Mannerist exaggerations appear, like the fantastic lion helmet of the famous 'Armure aux Lions' (Musée de l'Armée, Paris, G.50), made either for Francis I or for Henry II by Giovanni Paolo Negroli, but in general the suits are solid enough to be used in

Fig. 1
A three-quarter suit of armour made for Henry of Valois, decorated by Giovanni Paolo Negroli,
circa 1540–45
London £1,925,000 ($3,080,000). 5.V.83
From the collection of the Lord Astor of Hever

Fig. 2
A burgonet made for
Henry of Valois,
decorated by Giovanni
Paolo Negroli,
circa 1540–45
Reproduced courtesy of
the Département des
Objets d'Art, Musée du
Louvre, Paris

combat as well as for display on parade. The second group tends to be lighter and moves away from traditional shape and function towards more decorative 'Antique' forms: harnesses were sometimes modelled to emphasize the muscular anatomy of the human torso; the lower leg armour might be modelled to imitate intricately strapped sandals; and arm defences often disappear completely, except for the pauldrons, or shoulder pieces. The masters who excelled in this style worked in northern Italy, like Bartolommeo Campi of Pesaro, who made one of the most famous of them, a classical armour for Emperor Charles V (Armería Real, Madrid, A.188).

Common to both groups is their rich decoration. Foliate scrolls inhabited by monsters, masks and mythological figures animate the surfaces, emphasized by gilding on a blued ground, or silvering against a black ground. The decoration becomes increasingly rich and fantastic towards the mid-sixteenth century, and the plates are correspondingly thinner to enable the craftsmen to execute the intricate chasing and embossing. Even the earlier and heavier armours were showpieces, meant to be prominent and visible from a distance.

The Hever armour is one of the most elegantly deorated examples of the first group, suitable in theory for combat. Scrolling foliage issuing from grotesque bearded heads grows over the whole suit without disturbing the martial form. The outline of the decoration was embossed from the back and the sculptural detail was cut, chased, chiselled and finished from the front. To have done more from the back would have thinned the metal and reduced its efficacy as a defence. The decoration is nevertheless bold and crisp, which is a tribute to the unique skill of the artist.

Fig. 3
Henry of Valois, on panel, 10⅝in by 8¾in (27cm by 22.2cm)
Reproduced courtesy of the National Trust, Upton House, Warwickshire

There is a companion portrait of Francis I at Upton House, and both pictures have been attributed to the atelier of François Clouet, who became court painter in 1541.

Fig. 4
The helmet from the Hever armour

Fig. 5
The 'Duc de Guise' helmet, *circa* 1540–45
Reproduced courtesy of the Metropolitan Museum
of Art, New York (Purchase, Rogers Fund and
Gift of George D. Pratt, 1926)

Fig. 6
The breastplate from the Hever armour

Fig. 7
The 'Duc de Guise' breastplate, *circa* 1540–45
Reproduced courtesy of the Metropolitan Museum
of Art, New York (Gift of William H. Riggs, 1913)

The quality and style of the decoration point to a North Italian workshop. Among these, that of the numerous Negroli family in Milan was the most famous. The standard of their work and their decorative ingenuity brought them commissions from some of the most important royal and princely courts in Europe: examples of their work can still be found in the Bargello, Florence (for Guidobaldo II of Urbino), in Madrid (for Emperor Charles V), and in the Louvre and the Musée de l'Armée in Paris (for Cosimo de'Medici, Francis I and Henry II). The association with the French court is recorded to have been particularly close. According to the French courtier and historian of manners, the Seigneur de Brantôme (1540–1614), one of the Negroli spent some fifteen years in Paris. The meticulous accounts of Francis I record the commission of an extensive garniture from Nicolo Negroli and his workshop in 1525. This was still not paid for after 1530. The craftsmen included a brother and four sons of Nicolo Negroli, among them Giovanni Paolo, who later proved to be the most talented master in the family.

By about 1535, Giovanni Paolo (*circa* 1510–after 1565) was taking personal commissions and there is little doubt that he built and decorated the Armure aux Lions, mentioned above, for Francis I. With his brothers he also worked on a large garniture for Emperor Charles V (Armería Real, Madrid, A.139–46). The grotesque masks on this garniture are strikingly similar to those on the Hever armour and the lion masks on the Armure aux Lions. Several elbow cops made as exchange pieces are decorated with foliate scrolls that are unmistakably by the same hand as those on the Hever suit.

Sir Guy Francis Laking, who first described the Hever suit in his *Record of European Armour and Arms* (1920), observed the similarities with pieces attributed to the Negroli. He felt that the superficial treatment of some of the plates was not consistent with the quality expected from this workshop, but he suggested that the suit might have been made in France and decorated by an Italian craftsman. This would not be unusual. Furthermore, the outline of the suit is French, and the weak execution of technical details, like the turnover edges of some plates and the careless decoration on the border of the body armour, has parallels in other parade suits made in France.

As for the decorating craftsman, the connections with Giovanni Paolo Negroli are confirmed by a helmet and breastplate en suite, supposedly commissioned for the Duc de Guise. By the time they were made, Filippo and Giovanni Paolo Negroli were apparently so famous that they sometimes signed their work, a very rare occurrence; the breastplate carries the words: *IO PAULUS DE NEGROLIS ME FECIT*. Although the designs of the Hever and Guise breastplates are different (Figs 6–7), and the overloaded surfaces of the one seem to stand in direct contrast to the bold and elegantly spaced foliage on the other, there are strong similarities in the distribution and finish of the decoration; and there is also the same superficiality, especially in the etching, that disturbed Laking about the Hever armour. When one turns to the two helmets (Figs 4–5), the comparison is still more striking. Both have nearly the same outline and each is decorated with scrolling foliage by the same hand. The different crests, a mythological monster on the Guise helmet and a bearded mask on the Hever helmet, are both chiselled and undercut with the same skill.

The royal owner, the attribution to Giovanni Paolo Negroli and the improbability that a further suit by this maker, or any of the Negroli family, will ever appear on the market, explain the particular fascination of this historic armour.

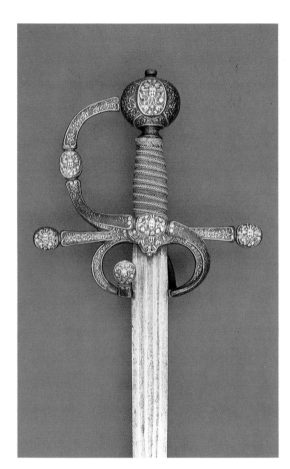

Left
An English riding sword, early seventeenth century, the grip eighteenth century,
length 38¼in (97.2cm)
London £33,000 ($52,800). 5.V.83
From the collection of the Lord Astor of Hever

This must be the finest English sword of its period recorded; the damascening and silver incrustation are preserved in exceptional condition. According to tradition, it was presented by Elizabeth I to a member of the Weatherby family.

Below
A naval presentation sword with enamel plaques, by John Ray and James Montague, London, 1800,
length 35¼in (89.5cm)
London £20,900 ($33,440). 3.III.83

Jerimiah Coghlan (1775?–1844), commander of the cutter *Viper*, was presented with this sword for capturing the French gun-brig *Cerbère* on 29 July 1800. It is engraved *A Tribute of Friendship from Admiral the EARL of St VINCENT to the INTREPID COGHLAN* and *Cerbere 29. July 1800.*

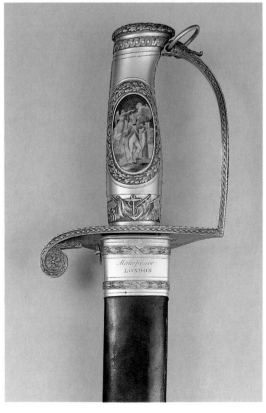

Opposite
A Flemish three-quarter suit of armour by the Master of the Snails and Dragonflies, first quarter seventeenth century, probably Antwerp
London £330,000 ($528,000). 5.V.83
From the collection of the Lord Astor of Hever

Henry Wriothesley, 3rd Earl of Southampton (1573–1624), Shakespeare's patron, was the first owner of this armour: there is a portrait of him with it in the collection of the late 7th Duke of Portland. The armour was probably acquired during Southampton's military service in the Low Countries against the Spanish.

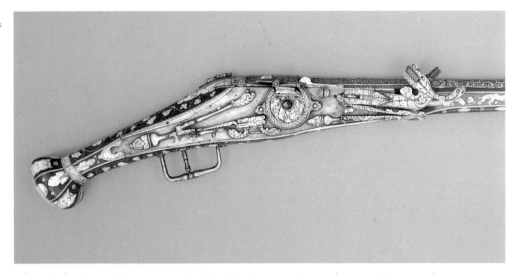

A breech-loading self-spanning wheel-lock holster pistol, Augsburg, mid-sixteenth century, length 30½in (77.5cm)
London £55,000 ($88,000). 5.V.83
From the collection of the Lord Astor of Hever

The technical refinements of this pistol are unique for its date.

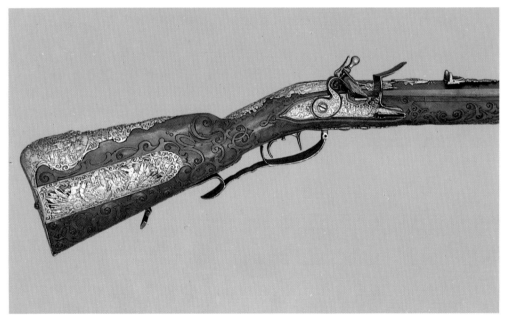

A flintlock rifle decorated with cast and chased gilt bronze and silver, by Joseph Nies, Mindelheim, *circa* 1740, length 36¼in (92.1cm)
London £29,700 ($47,520). 5.V.83
From the collection of the Lord Astor of Hever

This rifle is one of a pair made for Carl Albrecht, Elector of Bavaria (1726–45), later Holy Roman Emperor, Charles VII. The other is in the Bayerisches Nationalmuseum, Munich, where there are two further firearms made by Joseph Nies for the Electors of Bavaria.

Left
A db 8-bore hammer non-ejector wildfowling gun by
J. Purdey,
serial number 9807, 1877
London £2,530 ($4,048).
12.IV.83

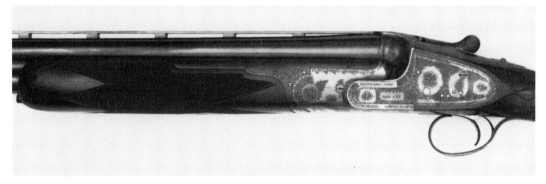

An over-and-under 12-bore assisted-opening sidelock ejector trap gun by Boss & Co.,
serial number 8990, 1953
London £9,350 ($14,960). 7.XII.82

Left
One of a pair of 'Modèle de
Luxe' db 12-bore self-opening
detachable sidelock ejector
sporting guns by Holland &
Holland,
serial numbers 36817/36818,
1967
London £19,800 ($31,680).
7.XII.82

Works of art

A limestone impost block, probably from the Abbey of St Denis workshop, after 1144,
width 32in (81.3cm)
New York $48,400 (£30,250). 10.VI.83
From the collection of the Glencairn Museum, Bryn Athyn, Pennsylvania; and now in The Cloisters,
Metropolitan Museum of Art, New York

This block is very similar to those in the ambulatory of the crypt of St Denis, built by Abbot Suger
(1122–51). Traces of paint suggest that it was once part of the fabric of the church.

A Catalonian polychrome wood relief figure of Christ in Majesty, from a group of seven figures, including five apostles and a seated king, originally part of an altar frontal, twelfth century, height 17½in (44.5cm)
New York $47,300 (£29,563). 3.XII.82

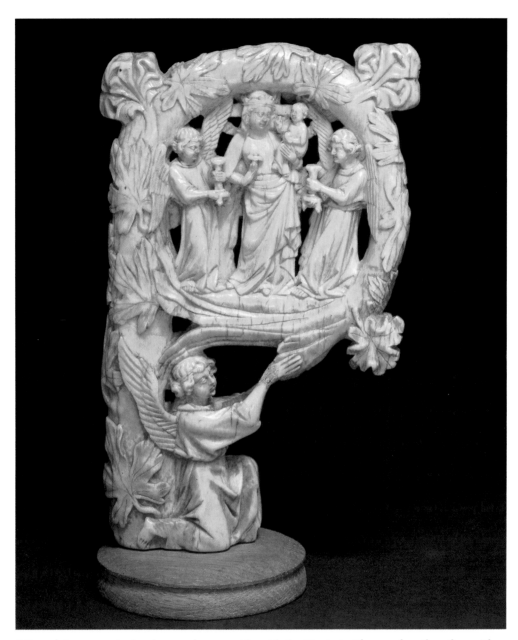

A French ivory crozier head, carved on one side with the Virgin in Glory and on the other with
the Crucifixion, second half fourteenth century, height 7in (17.8cm)
London £154,000 ($246,400). 6.V.83
From the collection of the Lord Astor of Hever

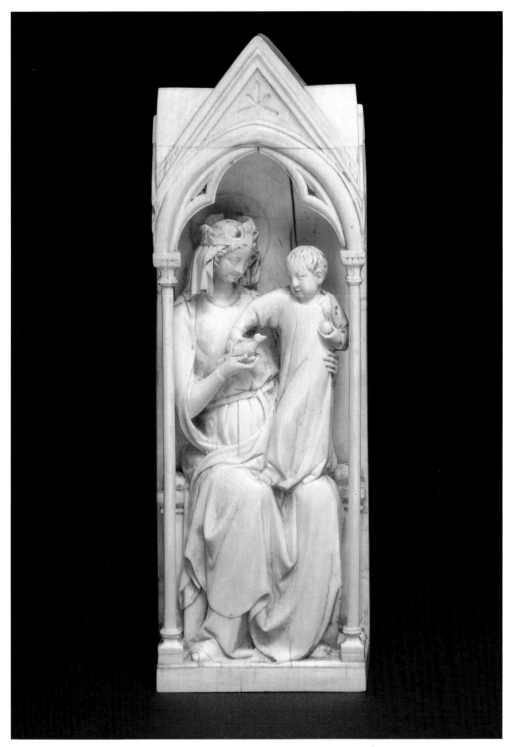

An ivory panel of the Virgin and Child from the centre of a polyptych, Île-de-France,
early fourteenth century, height $7\frac{7}{8}$ in (20cm)
London £28,600 ($45,760). 6.V.83
From the collection of the Lord Astor of Hever

The St Eustace casket from Hever Castle

Laila Zamuelis Gross

Seldom have the appealing qualities of ivory – its creamy whiteness, soft yet cool to the eye, its sensuousness to the touch – been better conveyed than by the St Eustace casket from the Hever Castle Collection (Fig. 1). The deep, gracefully rounded carving tells the story expressively and elegantly: under the undulating garments, the bodies are vigorous; every gesture is so delineated that it speaks to us even if we are not familiar with the legend depicted. Besides unusual expressiveness and vivacity, the carving also has that special quality so admired in the Middle Ages, *douceur*, for which the modern French retains the original connotations. The superb execution of this casket suggests the hand of a master craftsman and artist (the two were not considered separate in the Middle Ages) in Paris, around 1325.

Ivory has always been prized, but never more so than in the fourteenth century, when objects from the French ivory workshops were often simply referred to as *articles de Paris* and everyone, from kings to tradesmen, seems to have wanted as many kinds as possible. The workshops produced both religious and secular pieces in tremendous quantities. Because of the unique attributes of the material many ivory carvings survive, compared with other art forms from the Middle Ages: unlike precious materials ivory cannot be melted down, refashioned, reset or even easily recarved; it cannot be used for other functions or purposes, as wood or parchment can. It is pleasing and special enough to be kept even when fashions change, yet not precious enough to be coveted for the intrinsic value of the material itself.

According to the strict rules of the guilds, ivory was to be adorned only with precious materials and stones; consequently, few of the most elaborate objects de-scribed in inventories have come down to us. Given the superior workmanship of this casket, it probably had bands of gold or silver with precious stones (the mountings on it now are later additions). Miraculously the casket was not smashed to pieces, as they usually were, in the effort to obtain the precious materials. The almost pristine condition of the Hever casket seems to indicate that it was treasured and kept with great care. Although its provenance before the nineteenth century is lost in history, the conjectures made at that time may have been grounded in fact; namely that the casket had been in royal or aristocratic collections and had very few owners.

The subject matter of the casket points to the interests of the French aristocracy. The legend is the stuff of romances and of a type that was particularly beloved in the

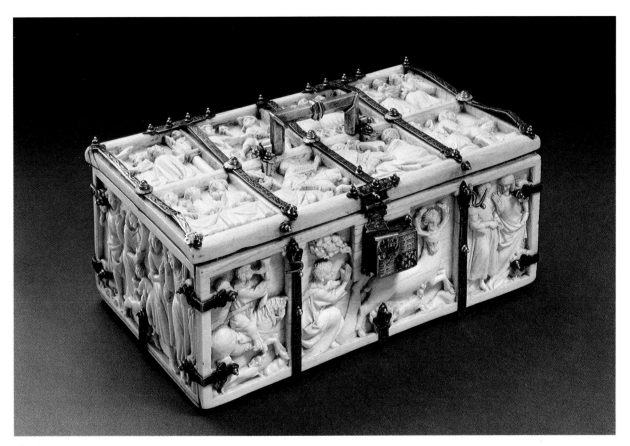

Fig. 1
A French Gothic ivory casket with scenes from the life of St Eustace, Paris, *circa* 1325,
width 6¾in (17.2cm)
London £418,000 ($668,800). 6.V.83
From the collection of the Lord Astor of Hever

Fig. 2
The front of the casket

Middle Ages: of the tribulations, separation and reunion of a family. The front panel
(Fig. 2) shows the Roman nobleman Placidus on a hunt – that most aristocratic of
pastimes so passionately pursued in the Middle Ages; next we see him in the familiar
pose of worship, before the stag between whose horns speaks the head of Christ. In
the last scene he tells his wife that they have to be baptized and she indicates that she
has had a dream about it. The right end of the casket (Fig. 3) depicts the almsgiving –
feeding and clothing the poor – that Placidus and his wife had engaged in even before
knowing Christ; in the adjoining scene a bishop baptizes the family. As a result,

Fig. 3
The right end of the casket

Fig. 4
The back of the casket

Placidus takes the new name of Eustace. Christ had said he was to be a second Job, and on the back panel (Fig. 4) we see the now penniless family leaving the plague-ridden city of Rome; next, Eustace is pushed ashore because he cannot pay the passage and the captain has taken a strong fancy to his wife, Theospis. One of the sons is then carried off by a lion, while on the left end of the casket (Fig. 5), Eustace watches his other son being snatched by a wolf, as a stream separates them. What he does not know, but what the texts tell and the carver carefully indicates is that farmers with clubs and pitchforks rescue the children. The top of the casket reads

Fig. 5
The left end of the casket

Fig. 6
The top of the casket

from bottom right to left (Fig. 6). A new emperor has sent out searchers for the great knight Placidus (Eustace) to help in his wars. Eustace is recognized by a scar on his head, then takes part in a battle, and is feasted at a banquet. The end comes quickly on the top, reading from left to right. Because Eustace refuses to pray to the idol that the emperor adores, he is placed with his reunited family in a fiery brazen bull. His sainthood is proclaimed in the last scene. The feast day of St Eustace is 20 September.

The legend is told forcefully and economically by the master carver. While many scenes and gestures are the standard, set scenes, part of the ivory carver's repertoire – the hunt, the joust and Eustace on his knees, precisely as a Magi or a lover would be – there are an unusual number of unique scenes and depicted objects for which the carver may not have had models at hand; the giving of alms, the recognition scene, the abduction scenes and the farmers' rescue, among others. Especially impressive in these invented scenes is the regard for minutely carved detail.

The legend is indisputably aristocratic, dealing with a brave knight, a beautiful lady and hunting. The interest in St Eustace in France is also particularly tied to royalty. The saint's body is reported to have been brought from Italy by an unspecified king in the twelfth century; it was richly enshrined in the Abbey of St Denis – a church special to the royal family and the final resting place for many French kings.

Later a queen acquired the saint's chin. A thirteenth-century *Vie de Saint Eustache*
reports the wonderful events:

> Ung roy françois par revelation
> A Romme fut, ainsy que l'en opine,
> Et la oyst faire relation
> Des dictz corps sainctz, dont tost vers eulx chemine,
> Priant a Dieu qui de tout determine,
> Qu'il luy octroit le corps du dict vaincqueur
> Pour l'emporter en France de bon coeur,
> Et a ce mot tous les tombeaulx se ouvrirent.
> Dont le dict corps de sainct Eustace misrent
> En ung cercoeul moult riche et precïux,
> Puys doulcement les chasses reclouyrent
> Aux benoictz sainctz et martirs glorïeux.
>
> Le corps en est sans quelque fiction
> A Sainct Denis de France, ou il recline,
> Et le menton par grand devotion
> Fut apporté par une noble royne
> A l'hospital sainct Jacques

(Deux Versions de la Vie de Saint Eustache en vers Français du Moyen Age, ed.
Holger Petersen [Dyggve] (Helsingfors, 1925), vv. 1232–45)

The relics at St Denis were destroyed by the Huguenots in the sixteenth century.

This excited emphasis on the connections with royalty is found in most versions of
the legend. Fourteen verse and prose 'Lives' of St Eustace survive in French from the
thirteenth to the fifteenth centuries. This is an unusually large number and attests to
the great popularity of the saint. We know also that there were plays about his life,
which have not survived, and probably other poems. Thus his popularity in French
medieval art is not at all surprising. Although no other ivory carving of St Eustace
approaches the quality of the Hever casket, among others, there is a casket with the
saint's life in the Victoria and Albert Museum in London, and on the lid of another in
the Louvre, Eustace appears in the company of the three most popular saints of the
Middle Ages: Christopher, Martin and George. Very appropriately, St Eustace's life is
also carved on medieval hunting horns, and his story is told in elaborate stained glass
in the cathedral of Chartres, as well as at the cathedrals of Sens, Mans and others.

St Eustace, not surprisingly, was the patron saint of aristocrats and those catering
to them, hunters and furriers. Members of the royalty and aristocracy were passionate
hunters and the only ones, by decree, permitted to wear expensive furs. In fact, the
very fine, large window at Chartres depicting the life of St Eustace was commissioned
and paid for by the guild of furriers and drapers.

St Eustace is a particularly 'secular' saint: his legend has many non-hagiographic
analogues in medieval literature and the emphasis on hunting reminds one of the
pleasures of this world (although there are the motifs of the Divine Stag and God as
the hunter in medieval thought). The casket was probably secular too in its use, since
such caskets usually held jewellery. However, their use as reliquaries is also attested.

An upper Rhine walnut relief of the Death of the Virgin, Alsace, *circa* 1410–30, width 34⅝in (88cm)
London £44,000 ($70,400). 10.III.83

Opposite
A Franconian polychrome limewood figure of St Sebastian, from the workshop of Tilmann
Riemenschneider, *circa* 1510, height 37⅝in (95.6cm)
London £31,900 ($51,040). 10.III.83

A *verre eglomisé* pax of the Virgin and Child with
St Antony Abbot and St Francis, possibly Lombard or
Tuscan, second half fifteenth century, height 4½in (11.5cm)
London £4,620($7,392). 10.III.83

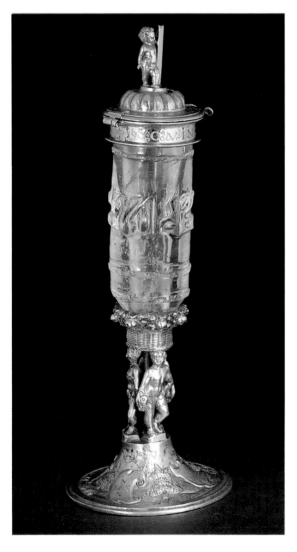

Left
A silver-gilt and carved rock-crystal reliquary, inscribed
IN HOC SIGNO VINCES, the Spanish mounts sixteenth
century, the Fatimid rock crystal tenth century,
height 7in (17.8cm)
London £28,600($45,760). 6.V.83
From the collection of the Lord Astor of Hever

A jewelled gold and enamel necklace suspending the device of the Order of the Golden Fleece,
possibly Prague, early seventeenth century
London £37,400 ($59,840). 6.V.83
From the collection of the Lord Astor of Hever

A Florentine bronze group of Angelica and Medoro, attributed to Ferdinando Tacca,
seventeenth century, height 16¼in (41.2cm)
New York $33,000 (£20,625). 10.VI.83

A South German ivory relief of the Rape of the Sabines, attributed to Ignaz Elhafen, after Pietro da Cortona, early eighteenth century, width 7in (17.8cm)
London £15,400 ($24,640). 10.III.83

Two views of an ivory cylinder for holding a tankard decorated with Bacchanalian scenes, by Bernard Strauss, signed and dated *1656*, Augsburg,
height 4in (10.2cm)
London £41,800 ($66,880). 6.V.83
From the collection of the Lord Astor of Hever

A marble group of the Three Graces by Jean-Baptiste
Carpeaux, signed, *circa* 1874, height $31\frac{7}{8}$in (81cm)
Monte Carlo FF 149,850 (£12,405:$19,848). 27.VI.83

Left
A bronze figure of a Saracen by Henri Plé, signed,
circa 1870, height $39\frac{1}{2}$in (100.3cm)
London £9,020 ($14,432). 25.XI.82

A bronze group of an Arabian lion hunter and his hounds, signed *WAACEPT Sc.*, *circa* 1870,
height of group 46¾in (118.7cm)
London £11,000 ($17,600). 25.XI.82

An icon of the Mother of God 'Hodegetria', Moscow, late fifteenth century, $9\frac{7}{8}$in by 8in (25cm by 20.2cm)
London £6,050($9,680). 21.II.83

A Cretan icon of the Virgin, sixteenth century, 12¾in by 9⅝in (32.4cm by 24.6cm)
London £16,500 ($26,400). 21.II.83

Representations of the Virgin without the Christ Child are rare.

A Fabergé purpurine figure of a cat, St Petersburg, *circa* 1900, height 5in (12.8cm)
New York $50,600(£31,625). 16.XII.82

Opposite
Above A Fabergé amethyst and diamond brooch, workmaster August Hollming, St Petersburg, late nineteenth
century, width 1in (2.4cm). SFr 7,920(£2,364:$3,782)
Centre, from left to right A jewelled, gold and enamel Easter egg pendant, *circa* 1900, height $\frac{3}{4}$in (1.8cm).
SFr 2,860(£854:$1,366)
A Fabergé jewelled, gold Easter egg pendant, workmaster August Holmström, St Petersburg, *circa* 1900,
height $\frac{5}{8}$in (1.7cm). SFr 2,200(£657:$1,051)
A Fabergé gold and purpurine Easter egg pendant, late nineteenth century, height $\frac{5}{8}$in (1.7cm).
SFr 4,180(£1,248:$1,997)
A jewelled, gold and enamel Easter egg pendant, maker's mark of Alexander Tillander, late nineteenth century,
height $\frac{3}{4}$in (1.9cm). SFr 3,300(£985:$1,576)
A Fabergé gold and rhodonite Easter egg pendant, workmaster August Hollming, *circa* 1900,
height $\frac{5}{8}$in (1.7cm). SFr 4,950(£1,478:$2,365)
Below A collection of twenty-three jewelled, gold and enamel Easter egg pendants.
SFr 26,400(£7,881:$12,610)

The brooch and Easter eggs illustrated on the opposite page were sold in Geneva on 11 May 1983.

From left to right
A silver-gilt and shaded enamel three-handled cup commemorating the Romanov tercentenary
(1613–1913), workmaster Pavel Ovchinnikov, Moscow, height 9in (23cm)
Geneva SFr 66,000 (£19,701:$31,522). 11.V.83
A silver-gilt and shaded enamel vase, maker's mark *S.V.*, Moscow, 1896, height $7\frac{7}{8}$in (20cm)
Geneva SFr 49,500 (£14,776:$23,642). 11.V.83

One of a pair of German mother-of-pearl and gold wall panels, with inset Augsburg enamel plaques, based on prints after the manner of Georg Philipp Rugendas, the enamels *circa* 1705, the panels probably later, width 16in (40.5cm)
London £27,500 ($44,000). 4.VII.83

Opposite, left
A gilt-metal and enamel nef, Vienna, late nineteenth century, height 47in (119.4cm)
New York $40,700 (£25,438). 17.XII.82
From the collection of the late Wilfred Swall

Opposite, right
A gilt-metal paste-set automaton carillon repeating double-dialled clock for the Oriental market, late eighteenth century, height of clock 38in (96.5cm)
New York $39,600 (£24,750). 16.III.83

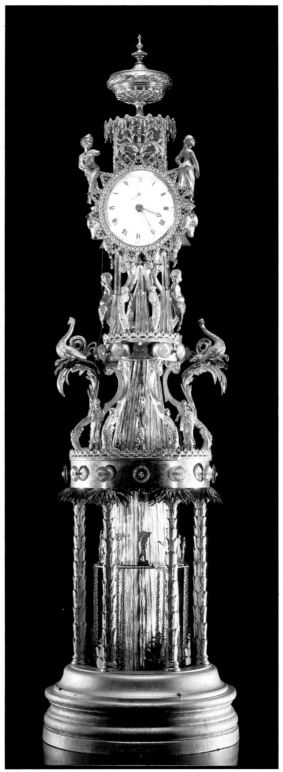

A jewelled, gold and enamel musical singing-bird box, maker's mark of Jean-George Rémond & Co., Geneva, 1807–14, width 3⅛in (8cm)
Geneva SFr85,800(£25,612:$40,979). 11.V.83

A Swiss gold and enamel snuff box, maker's mark probably *F J*, *circa* 1770, width 3¾in (9.5cm)
Geneva SFr 55,000(£16,418:$26,269). 26.XI.82

This box is painted with genre scenes based on prints after Fragonard.

Two views of a gold presentation *boîte à miniatures*, inset with miniatures by Van Blarenberghe, the lid signed and dated *1768*, maker's mark of Ange-Joseph Aubert, Paris, 1767–68, width 3⅛in (8cm) London £110,000 ($176,000). 4.VII.83
From the collection of the Comte Antoine de Dreux-Brézé

Aubert first entered his mark on 26 July 1762 and later served as jeweller to the crown. According to family tradition, this snuff box was presented by Louis XV to his cousin the Prince de Tingry on the occasion of his third marriage, to Eléanore-Josèphe-Pulchérie des Laurents. The top of the box shows a village kermesse with peasants dancing to a double-bass and a hurdy-gurdy, while on the base there is a *bal masqué* in a parkland glade, lit by chandeliers and sconces hanging from the trees.

SAMUEL COOPER
Oliver Cromwell, on
vellum, signed and dated
1649, $2\frac{1}{4}$in (5.8cm)
London £25,300 ($40,480).
4.VII.83

Right
LAURENCE HILLIARD
A gentleman aged seventy-four,
on vellum, dated *1621*,
$2\frac{1}{8}$in (5.4cm)
London £19,800 ($31,680).
11.VII.83
From the collection of
Mrs Daphne Foskett

NICHOLAS HILLIARD
A lady, on vellum, *circa* 1590,
$2\frac{1}{8}$in (5.4cm)
London £19,250 ($30,800). 11.VII.83
From the collection of the
Lord Astor of Hever

STUDIO OF JOHN HOSKINS
Charles II as a boy, on vellum,
circa 1638, $3\frac{1}{4}$in (8.3cm)
London £12,100 ($19,360). 15.XI.82

ISAAC OLIVER after HANS HOLBEIN
THE YOUNGER
Sir Nicholas Poyntz aged twenty-five,
on vellum, *circa* 1595, $3\frac{1}{4}$in (8.3cm)
London £6,380 ($10,208). 7.III.83
From the collection of
Sir Valentine Abdy, Bt

NATHANIEL HONE
A young lady, enamel, signed and
dated *1749*, 1⅞in (4.8cm)
London £2,860 ($4,576). 4.VII.83

Attributed to the
HUAUD BROTHERS
A lady, enamel, *circa* 1690,
1⅛in (3cm)
Geneva SFr 17,600
(£5,254:$8,406). 11.V.83

JOHN SMART
Mrs Baker, signed and dated
1783, 2in (5.2cm)
London £7,700 ($12,320).
4.VII.83

THOMAS RICHMOND
A gentleman, possibly Thomas
Molineaux, *circa* 1810, 2⅝in (6.6cm)
London £7,590 ($12,144). 4.VII.83
From the collection of
Mrs Mercedes Antonia Lewis

JEAN-BAPTISTE AUGUSTIN
A lady, enamel, *circa* 1800, 3⅛in (8cm)
Geneva SFr 22,000 (£6,567:$10,507). 11.V.83

Clocks and watches

A gilt-metal table clock with calendar, probably Augsburg, 1580,
height $8\frac{1}{2}$ in (21.5cm)
Florence L 39,200,000 (£16,436 : $26,298). 26.V.83

Opposite
A Directoire month mantel regulator with calendar and equation of time by
Jean-Antoine Lépine , Paris, *circa* 1795, height $18\frac{1}{2}$ in (47cm)
London £30,800 ($49,280). 21.X.82

Jean-Antoine Lépine was received Master in 1762 and worked for some years as a
clockmaker to the king.

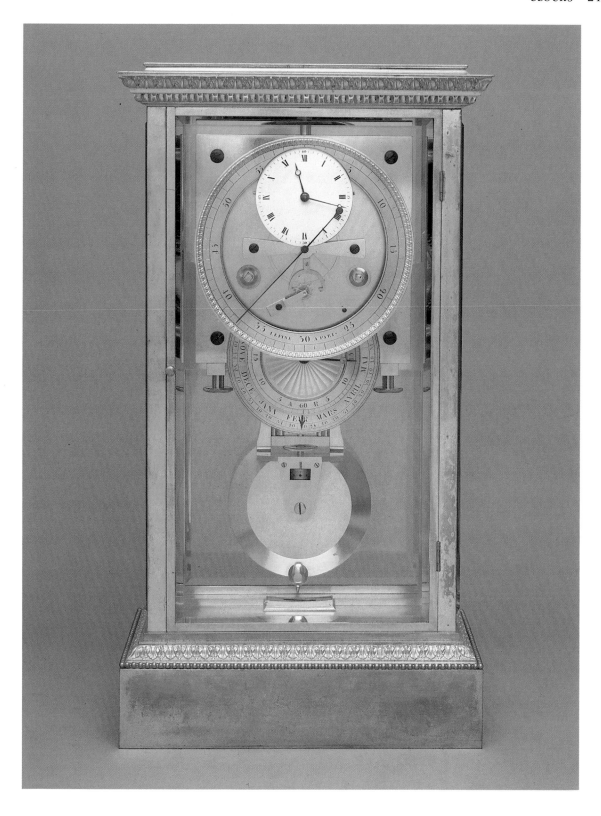

BREGUET NO. 3101
A gold cased quarter-repeating alarum
watch with Robin escapement, Paris,
diameter $2\frac{1}{4}$in (5.8cm)
London £15,400 ($24,640). 24.II.83

BREGUET NO. 3917
A gold and silver cased *première classe*
half-quarter-repeating lever watch, Paris,
diameter $1\frac{7}{8}$in (4.8cm)
London £13,200 ($21,120). 24.II.83

BREGUET NO. 3358
A silver half-quarter-repeating
eight-day carriage clock with
calendar and alarum, Paris,
1826, height $5\frac{5}{8}$in (14.2cm)
Geneva SFr 154,000
(£45,970: $73,552). 26.XI.82
From the collection of
Edward Hornby

Left
GEORGE MARGETTS
NO. 312
A silver cased
astronomical
cylinder watch,
London, 1813,
diameter
$2\frac{5}{8}$in (6.6cm)
London £22,000
($35,200). 24.II.83

Right
A gold, enamel, pea[r]
and diamond cased
sweep-seconds
virgule watch and
châtelaine for the
Oriental market,
circa 1800,
diameter of watch
$2\frac{1}{4}$in (5.8cm)
New York $16,500
(£10,313). 6.X.82

Below, left
JAMES WILLIAM BENSON NO. 3217
A gold hunting cased minute-repeating keyless lever clockwatch
with perpetual calendar, London, 1897, diameter $2\frac{1}{2}$in (6.2cm)
New York $49,500(£30,938). 8.XII.82

Below, right
JAMES McCABE NO. 08400
A gold keyless lever minute-repeating *grande* and *petite sonnerie*
clockwatch, London, 1889, diameter $2\frac{1}{4}$in (5.8cm)
Geneva SFr 77,000(£22,985:$36,776). 26.XI.82

PATEK PHILIPPE NO. 888046
A perpetual calendar wristwatch, 1961,
diameter 1½in (3.7cm)
London £6,490 ($10,384). 26.V.83

A gold automatic skeleton wristwatch by
Gerald Genta, retailed by Van Cleef & Arpels,
circa 1970, diameter 1¼in (3.2cm)
London £2,860 ($4,576). 26.V.83

AARON WILLARD JR NO. 2378
A Federal mahogany giltwood and *verre eglomisé* banjo clock
with alarum, Boston, *circa* 1820, height 40in (101.6cm)
New York $16,500 (£10,313). 23.X.82

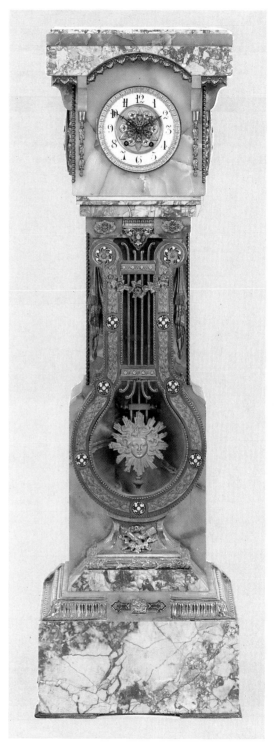

GUSTAVE BECKER NO. 397916
A porcelain-mounted pedestal clock, Vienna,
circa 1900, height 6ft 4½in (194.3cm)
London £12,100 ($19,360). 24.VI.83

A French marble, onyx and *champlevé* enamel
clock, *circa* 1890, height 4ft 5in (134.7cm)
London £6,380 ($10,208). 18.III.83

Musical instruments

A clavichord by Johann Adolph Hass, Hamburg, 1767, inscribed on the soundboard *J. A. Hass, Hambg. Anno 1767*, length 5ft 9½in (176.5cm)
London £13,750 ($22,000). 7.IV.83
From the collection of the late Mrs M. J. A. Russell

Opposite, left
An ivory-backed theorbo, the body, soundboard and first neck early seventeenth century, the rest and some decoration late nineteenth century, labelled *Tomas Spilman in Venetia*,
length of body 20in (50.8cm)
London £5,720 ($9,152). 6.V.83
From the collection of the Lord Astor of Hever

Opposite, right
An ivory-backed six-course lute, stamped *H.D.* twice, length of body 18⅜in (46.7cm)
London £9,900 ($15,840). 6.V.83
From the collection of the Lord Astor of Hever

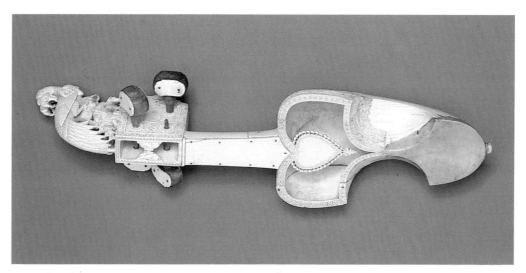

A North Indian ivory sarinda, *circa* 1800, length $22\frac{7}{16}$ in (57cm)
London £8,250 ($13,200). 6.V.83
From the collection of the Lord Astor of Hever

The sarinda is a folk instrument but this example is unusually ornate, suggesting that it was made for a North Indian court where both classical and folk musicians were employed.

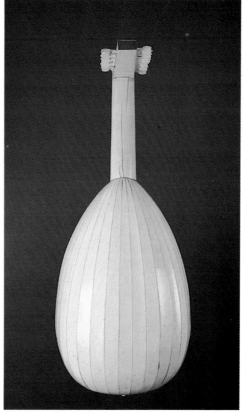

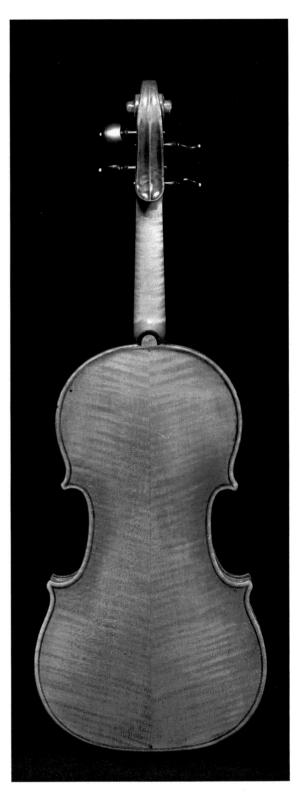

A violin by Peter Guarneri of Venice, 1750, labelled
*Petrus Guarnerius Filius Ioseph Cremonensis fecit
Venetijs. Anno 1750,*
length of back 13$\frac{15}{16}$in (35.4cm)
London £66,000 ($105,600). 4.XI.82

The Muir-Mackenzie violin by Antonio Stradivari,
Cremona, *circa* 1730, labelled *Antonius Stradivarius
Cremonensis Faciebat Anno 1722,*
length of back 14in (35.5cm)
New York $275,000 (£171,875). 13.VI.83

A violin by Antonio Stradivari, Cremona,
circa 1724, labelled *Antonius Stradiuarius
Cremonensis Faciebat Anno 1724*,
length of back 14in (35.5cm)
London £110,000 ($176,000). 23.VI.83

The ex-Briggs violin by Joannes Baptista
Guadagnini, Cremona, 1758, labelled *Joannes
Baptista Guadagnini fecit Cremonae 1758*,
length of back 14in (35.5cm)
London £79,200 ($126,720). 7.IV.83

Left, from left to right
A dancing master's kit, school of
Peter Walmsley, London, first half
eighteenth century,
total length 17⅛in (43.5cm)
London £550($880). 7.IV.83
A German pochette,
mid-seventeenth century,
length 16½in (41.9cm)
London £880($1,408). 7.IV.83

Right
A child's violin by Antonio
Stradivari, Cremona, 1720, labelled
*Antonius Stradiuarius Cremonensis
Faciebat Anno 1720 A.S.*,
length of back 10½in (26.7cm)
London £16,500($26,400). 7.IV.83

Only one other violin of this size by
Stradivari is known to survive. The
mould for his small instruments and
the paper patterns for the side
elevation and shield finial of both
surviving pieces are in the Ala
Ponzone Civic Museum, Cremona.

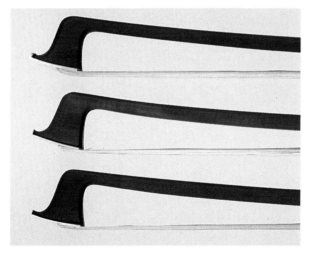

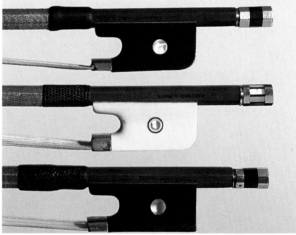

From top to bottom
A silver-mounted viola bow by Claude Thomassin, Paris, stamped *C. Thomassin a Paris*,
weight 72 grams. £1,760($2,816)
A gold and ivory-mounted viola bow by Eugène Sartory, Paris, stamped *E. Sartory a Paris*,
weight 73 grams. £4,840($7,744)
A silver-mounted viola bow by François-Nicolas Voirin, Paris, stamped *F. N. Voirin a Paris*,
weight 64 grams. £2,860($4,576)

The bows illustrated above were sold in London on 4 November 1982.

The Barbirolli violoncello by Gennaro Gagliano,
Naples, *circa* 1726, labelled *Januarius Gaglianus
Fecit Neapoli 1726*, length of back $29\frac{7}{16}$ in (74.8cm)
London £62,700 ($100,320). 7.IV.83
From the collection of Lady Barbirolli

The Barjansky violoncello by Antonio Stradivari,
Cremona, *circa* 1695, labelled *Antonius Stradiuarius
Cremonensis Faciebat Anno 1684*,
length of back $29\frac{7}{8}$ in (75.9cm)
London £192,500 ($308,000). 23.VI.83

Furniture and tapestries

A Chippendale shell-carved and block-front mahogany kneehole dressing table by the
Goddard-Townsend family, possibly Edmund Townsend, Newport, Rhode Island, *circa* 1765,
width 2ft 11in (88.9cm)
New York $687,500 (£429,688). 29.I.83

One of a pair of Federal swivel-top mahogany card tables attributed to Duncan Phyfe, New York, *circa* 1805, width 3ft (91.5cm)
New York $275,000 (£171,875). 30.VI.83

General John Cadwalader's 'hairy-paw-foot' furniture

Lita Solis-Cohen

After defeats by the British at Brandywine and Germantown had forced the Continental Army into winter quarters at Valley Forge, General Thomas Conway agitated for the removal from command of General George Washington. A young Pennsylvania Militia General named John Cadwalader challenged Conway to a duel. Cadwalader shot Conway in the face saying, 'Well I've stopped that damned lying mouth for a time anyway'. Thus Cadwalader in 1777 helped secure Washington's place in history.

If John Cadwalader had not had a town house filled with fine furniture, we might remember him only as the Revolutionary general who helped quash the Conway Cabal. But Cadwalader is best-known today for owning the finest furniture made by colonial craftsmen, including the most expensive chair ever sold at auction (Fig. 1).

Cadwalader, a third generation Philadelphian, was born in 1742. He and his brother attended the College of Philadelphia and finished their education with a grand tour, before settling down as dry goods merchants in their home town, then the second largest city in the English-speaking world. John Cadwalader presided over the jockey club, rode to hounds with the Gloucester Hunt, and was a member of the Summer Club, a fishing and eating club that met near the falls of the Schuylkill. He was also the best ice skater in Philadelphia.

As a zealous patriot, he signed the Non-Importation Agreement in 1765. He must have sympathized with Samuel Morris, who wrote in a letter to his nephew, Samuel Powel: 'Household goods may be had here as cheap and as well made from English patterns. In the humour people are in here, a man is in danger of becoming invidiously distinguished who buys anything in England which our tradesmen can furnish.'

In September 1768, John Cadwalader married an heiress, Elizabeth (Betsy) Lloyd of Maryland. The following year the young couple bought a nine-year-old house on South Second Street in Philadelphia, and spent the next two years redecorating the interior and furnishing it. Fortunately most of the bills and receipts for this work remain and were given by the Cadwalader family to the Historical Society of Philadelphia. In 1964, Nicholas Wainwright, then director of the society, wrote a delightful book, *Colonial Grandeur in Philadelphia, The House and Furniture of General John Cadwalader*, using the bills and receipts to portray the house and its furnishings.

By the winter of 1770–71 the carved mouldings, fireplace mantels and entablatures in the two large parlours were in place and painted, gold leaf had been applied to the

Fig. 1
A Chippendale serpentine-front mahogany 'hairy-paw-foot' chair, attributed to Thomas Affleck,
Philadelphia, *circa* 1770
New York $275,000 (£171,875). 23.X.82

papier-mâché borders and the ornamental plasterwork affixed to the ceilings. The Cadwaladers moved in with practically everything new. According to the bills, all but one piece of furniture was procured in Philadelphia; none of it was imported.

Cadwalader patronized the Philadelphia cabinetmakers Thomas Affleck, Benjamin Randolph and William Savery. From Affleck, whose shop was nearby on Second Street, he purchased two desks, a bedstead with castors, cornices for the windows, two sofas for the window recesses, a large sofa for the big parlour, an easy chair, two card tables, a tea table, a breakfast table, a night table, four firescreens, a harpsichord frame, a set of ten chairs for the front parlour, a set of ten chairs for the back parlour, and probably more. On 2 January 1771, Affleck billed Cadwalader for the '2 commode card tables at £5 a piece', and on the bottom of that bill are the names James Reynolds, Bernard and Jugiez with the note, 'Carving the Above'.

In the parlour were five portraits by Charles Willson Peale, which still survive. One portrays John's brother, Lambert, leaning on a ribbon-back chair resembling the one sold last October. The portrait of John himself with his wife and baby daughter shows the baby sitting on the celebrated serpentine-front card table (Fig. 2), which, with the portraits, remains in the Cadwalader family.

In addition to this table, Wainwright illustrated five pieces of Cadwalader furniture: a marble-top pier table with French scroll feet (now in the Metropolitan Museum of Art), a card table, looking glass and side chair (now at the H.F. du Pont Winterthur Museum in Delaware), and an easy chair owned by a Cadwalader descendant. All except the marble-top table have 'hairy-paw' feet derived from the lion's paw so carefully depicted in Chippendale's *Director*.

Since Wainwright wrote his book, further pieces of hairy-paw furniture have been discovered. Another serpentine card table was found in Canada and is now on loan to the Philadelphia Museum of Art. More dramatic was the appearance in London of five chairs with serpentine fronts, made to go with the serpentine card tables and matching a chair at Winterthur. They were brought to Sotheby's in 1973, and sold in November 1974 in New York for $207,000, then a record for a set of chairs.

This sale inspired yet another book about Cadwalader's furniture, *The Case of Major Fanshawe's Chairs* by David Loughlin, in which he tried to find out how and when John Cadwalader's chairs had got to London. Loughlin learned that they had been consigned by Major R.G. Fanshawe, who had inherited them from an old friend, Nancy Hone Connell, whose house was in Leixlip, County Kildare. Mrs Connell had purchased five chairs from the late Lord Westmeath's estate sale in 1934 for £19.

On two chairs, the signature *C. Hanlon, John Wannamaker's* [*sic*] *Phila* was found in pencil on the underside of the shoe – the piece of wood between the splat and the seat rail. This provided another clue. It proved that the chairs were in Philadelphia until after 1887, when John Wanamaker's, a men's furnishing store, expanded into a department store. But who was C. Hanlon? Loughlin found him listed as an upholsterer in the Philadelphia city directories from 1901 to 1905.

The chairs then may not have left Philadelphia until 1904. That date coincides with an auction of some of John Cadwalader's furniture by order of his great-grandson, Dr Charles Cadwalader, prior to his taking residence in Europe. The catalogue for his sale was known to Nicholas Wainwright, but has since been lost. According to Wainwright it listed 'Ten Handsom [*sic*] Antique Mahogany Chairs covered in canary satin damask'.

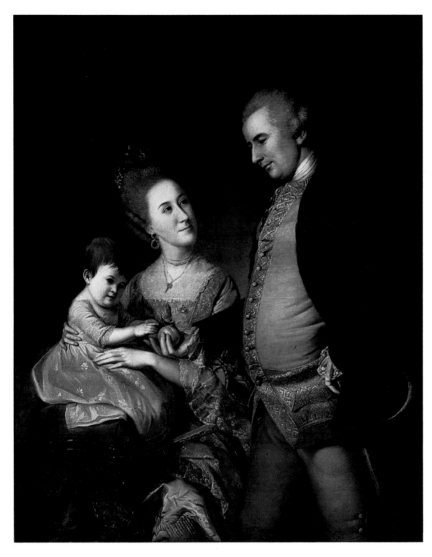

Fig. 2
CHARLES WILLSON PEALE
*Portrait of General John
Cadwalader, his wife Elizabeth
and their daughter Anne*
51in by 41in (129.5cm by 104cm)
Reproduced courtesy of
the owner

Were the 'Fanshawe Five' among the Cadwalader chairs sold in Philadelphia in 1904? Or were they perhaps taken abroad by Dr Cadwalader? It is also possible that the chairs left the family shortly after General John Cadwalader's death in 1786. Betsy Cadwalader had died in February 1776, and in 1779 Cadwalader was remarried to a noted beauty, Williamina Bond. Thomas and Frances Cadwalader, the children of his second marriage, subsequently inherited half of the Second Street property. So when Frances married David Montague Erskine, 2nd Lord Erskine, in 1799, and went to live with him in England, perhaps she took some of her father's chairs with her.

Thomas Cadwalader and Betsy's three daughters may also have inherited chairs. Loughlin believes that Lord Westmeath, who was attached to the British Embassy in Washington in 1897, may have visited Philadelphia, bought the chairs at Wana-maker's, and sent them home to Pallas Castle, County Galway. The fact that a 1913 inventory of Pallas lists '13 mahogany chairs covered in leather cloth' makes Loughlin suspect that there are eight more Cadwalader chairs in Britain.

Each of the Fanshawe chairs bears a number, 'VII' to 'XI', on its shoe, indicating that the set was a large one. Among the Cadwalader papers there is a bill from one Plunket Fleeson of October 1770, for 'covering over the rail finish'd in Canvis [*sic*] 32 chairs'. In an inventory of 1786, twenty chair cases are listed in a trunk in the garret, ten yellow and ten blue, matching the paint colours in the front and back parlours respectively. Philip D. Zimmerman, writing in the *Winterthur Portfolio 13* (1979), suggested that Cadwalader had a set of twenty hairy-paw chairs with serpentine fronts, divided between the front and back parlours, and a further set of twelve chairs with hairy-paw feet and straight fronts.

When another serpentine-front chair appeared at Sotheby's in October 1982, there was speculation about its history (Fig. 1). Catalogued as 'Property of a European Gentleman', it too had come from London to New York for sale. After tacks were removed from its leather covering, the number '*I*' was found branded on the seat rail and on the underside of the shoe. It was surely from Cadwalader's set.

Two paper labels pasted on the back seat rail provided the clue to its provenance; one, with a red border, inscribed in ink 'stored for Mrs E.R. Warrington', and the other a printed card reading, 'M.r and M.rs [*sic*] Samuel M. Scott'. Philadelphia Social Registers for the years 1898 to 1916 show that Mrs E.R. Warrington (born Frances Glen) became Mrs Samuel M. Scott in 1900, and that the couple lived in Italy after 1907. This suggests that chair number '*I*' had a different history from the Fanshawe Five, and that it left Philadelphia sometime between 1900 and 1907.

Frances Scott died in Florence in 1933 and Samuel died four months later on 29 January 1934, leaving in his will to 'Jenny Puccini, his maid servant of 22 years', 1,000 lire and the contents of her room. In addition to a chest of drawers, bedstead, blankets, towels and sheets, the will specified 'one mahogany chair'.

The Scott wills came to my attention after I had published a story in the *Philadelphia Inquirer*. I received a call from Clifford Lewis, 3rd, who identified himself as 'one of Fanny Scott's legatees', and offered to show me copies of Samuel and Frances Scott's wills. Lewis had known about the chair from a family note made in 1934, which described it as 'belonging to the David Lewis desk'. David Lewis was the grandfather of Frances Scott's mother, and a neighbour of the John Cadwaladers on Second Street. He may have bought or 'borrowed' the chair from Cadwalader's widow, or perhaps it was a gift when Williamina Cadwalader moved to smaller quarters.

A few weeks after the sale of Jenny Puccini's chair, an appraiser in Pittsburgh, Pennsylvania, valuing the furniture of the late Mrs G. David Thompson, discovered yet another previously unknown Cadwalader piece – a hairy-paw straight-front card table (Fig. 3). The table is identical to the Cadwalader card table at Winterthur and was probably made en suite with the set of straight-front hairy-paw chairs, four of which are in the Winterthur collection.

The table had been purchased by the late art collector and financier G. David Thompson from Charles Savage, an innkeeper and collector in Northeast Harbor, Maine. Savage had bought it from the estate of Beatrix Farrand, a great-great-granddaughter of John Cadwalader. The bill from Savage to Thompson, dated 1964, found among Thompson's papers, lists '1 English mahogany card table, $640'.

The quest for the rest of Cadwalader's furniture continues.

Fig. 3
A Chippendale straight-front mahogany 'hairy-paw-foot' card table, attributed to Thomas Affleck,
Philadelphia, *circa* 1770, width 32in (81cm)
New York $242,000(£151,250). 29.I.83
From the collection of the late Mrs G. David Thompson

A Louis XIV gilt-bronze-mounted brass and tortoiseshell-inlaid *bureau plat* in the manner of
André-Charles Boulle, early eighteenth century, width 4ft 3¼in (130.2cm)
New York $935,000 (£584,375). 7.V.83

There is an almost identical desk in the Musée Condé, Chantilly, and both are close in design to a
drawing in the Musée des Arts Décoratifs, Paris, attributed to André-Charles Boulle.

Opposite
A Louis XV gilt-wood armchair, *circa* 1765
London £28,050 ($44,880). 19.XI.82

This armchair, in early Neoclassical style, bears the mark of the Château de Chanteloup, which had
been built for the Duc de Choiseul.

A Louis XVI gilt-bronze-mounted lacquer secretaire cabinet attributed to Adam Weisweiler and made
for the king's study at Versailles, early 1780s, height 4ft 6¼in (137.8cm)
London £990,000 ($1,584,000). 8.VII.83

Two from a set of four Louis XVI gilt-bronze-mounted boulle cabinets signed by Etienne Levasseur, last quarter eighteenth century, height 3ft 2¼in (97cm)
New York $264,000 (£165,000). 7.V.83

Levasseur was probably trained by André-Charles Boulle II (1685–1745) and specialized in making furniture using the boulle technique. He was received Master in 1767. A similar pair of cabinets by this maker is in the collection of the Duke of Wellington at Stratfield Saye.

Opposite
In 1780 Louis XVI began to replace the unfashionable Louis XV furniture in his study, the inner sanctum of the royal apartments at Versailles. This cabinet corresponds exactly to the description of a black lacquer cabinet delivered by the *marchand-mercier* Dominique Daguerre in 1784. It was probably made by Adam Weisweiler, who had been received a Master *ébéniste* in Paris in 1778. He often worked for Daguerre, who had a virtual monopoly on the Oriental lacquer incorporated into furniture, like the seventeenth-century Japanese panels used here. The cabinet originally had a top of Spanish brocatelle marble. As the king's study already contained a roll-front writing desk and a flat-topped writing table, this piece of furniture was probably intended for storing papers.

Left
A Louis XIV
gilt-bronze-mounted
pewter and tortoiseshell
thermometer–barometer,
third quarter
seventeenth century,
height 4ft 2½in (128.2cm)
New York $71,500
(£44,688). 6.XI.82

Right
A Louis XIV gilt-bronze-mounted brass-inlaid tortoiseshell and
ebony clock attributed to André-Charles Boulle, height 10ft 8in (325cm)
Monte Carlo FF 1,443,000 (£119,454: $191,126). 26.VI.83
From the collection of the late Duchess Serra di Cassano

A similar clock, incorporated into the central part of an *armoire*, is in the
Wallace Collection, London.

A Venetian painted and gilt *bombé* commode, mid-eighteenth century, width 4ft 6in (137.1cm)
London £57,200 ($91,520). 15.VII.83

A Louis XV gilt-bronze-mounted black lacquer serpentine-front commode, stamped *B.V.R.B.*, width 4ft ⅜in (123cm)
Monte Carlo FF 1,665,000 (£137,831:$220,530). 13.II.83
Bernard van Risenburgh II was received Master before 1730.

One of a pair of George II burr-walnut concertina games tables, *circa* 1740, width 2ft 11½in (90.2cm)
New York $66,000 (£41,250). 23.IV.83

Opposite
A James I mahogany armchair, possibly Exeter, early seventeenth century
London £9,900 ($15,840). 22.X.82

The arms on this chair are those of Roope of Tunstall, Devon. The wood is Brazilian mahogany of the
Mimusopps species (also known as cherry mahogany or bullet wood), although mahogany was not
normally imported into England until after 1721. The chair was probably made from a batch of this
'red and peckled wood', recorded to have been imported through Dartmouth by Nicholas Roope from
the Portuguese colony on the Amazon. It came in return for a cargo of beads, knives, spades and
hatchets that he had sent out in 1617.

A George II painted and parcel-gilt looking glass in the manner of Thomas Chippendale, *circa* 1755, height 7ft 11in (241.3cm)
London £28,600 ($45,760). 8.IV.83

One of a pair of George II mahogany armchairs in the manner of Thomas Chippendale, *circa* 1755
London £66,000 ($105,600). 17.VI.83

A William IV mahogany partners' desk, *circa* 1825, width 6ft 2½in (189cm)
London £17,600($28,160). 12.XI.82

A Regency gilt-bronze-mounted mahogany Carlton House writing desk, early nineteenth century,
width 5ft 6in (167.5cm)
New York $55,000 (£34,375). 23.IV.83

Opposite
A Victorian mahogany extending dining table, stamped *Johnstone Jupe & Co., New Bond St.,
London 13399, circa* 1840, diameter closed 5ft 6in (167.5cm)
London £35,200 ($56,320). 17.VI.83

A Louis XV style gilt-bronze-mounted fruitwood-inlaid purplewood marquetry *bureau plat*, Paris,
late nineteenth century, width 6ft 2in (188cm)
New York $44,000 (£27,500). 29.X.82

This bureau is a copy of that made for Louis XVI in 1786, to match the *Bureau du Roi* commissioned by
Louis XV from Jean-François Oeben and Jean-Henri Riesener. It is stamped *NZ* on two mounts.

Opposite
Two from a set of four Florentine bronze torchères, *circa* 1880, height of each 11ft 2in (340cm)
London £35,200 ($56,320). 18.III.83

A pair of German Renaissance style silver throne chairs, possibly Hanau, *circa* 1880
London £14,300 ($22,880). 24.VI.83
From the collection of the Lord Astor of Hever

A Louis XIV style gilt-wood centre table, *circa* 1880, width 5ft 9in (175.2cm)
London £11,550 ($18,480). 18.III.83

A Louis XVI style gilt-bronze guéridon, *circa* 1880, height 2ft 5in (73.6cm) London £8,800 ($14,080). 18.III.83

A Régence style gilt-bronze-mounted kingwood and tulipwood parquetry regulator, stamped *BY* for Alfred Beurdeley, Paris, late nineteenth century, height 8ft 11in (271.8cm) New York $35,750 (£22,344). 29.X.82

Detail of a panoramic wallpaper, *The voyages of Captain Cook*, twenty-one panels,
each panel 6ft 6¾in by 1ft 8⅞in (200cm by 53cm)
Monte Carlo FF299,700 (£24,810:$39,696). 14.II.83
Now in the Australian National Gallery, Canberra

One of the rarest French wallpapers, *Les sauvages de la Mer Pacifique*, known in English as *The voyages of Captain Cook*, was manufactured at Mâcon *circa* 1805 by Joseph Dufour (1752–1827), from the designs of Jean-Gabriel Charvet (1750–1829). The composition was based upon published accounts of Cook's voyages, their accompanying engravings after the drawings of John Webber and William Hodges, and two popular dramas: *Omai, or a Trip round the World*, and *La Mort du Capitaine Cook*, performed in Paris in 1788. Dufour's declared intention was to produce a visual survey of the islands of the Pacific, but the result is somewhat more modest, featuring among other elements, the people of Nootka Sound visited by Cook in 1778, and his death the following year in Hawaii. Unpleasantness is not allowed to detract from the serene mood.

It is perhaps curious that this subject was considered appropriate at a time of rivalry between England and France. However, under Napoleon the French were keenly interested in Pacific exploration. Nicolas Baudin's expedition, which returned in 1804, may have refocused attention upon the achievements of the English explorer thirty years earlier. Furthermore, the South Seas seemed to provide a perfect example of Jean-Jacques Rousseau's 'natural paradise' and the 'noble savage'. Dufour stated in a promotional pamphlet for the wallpaper that, as well as being a history, geography and botany lesson it would, 'assist in creating by means of new comparisons, a community of taste and enjoyment between those who live in a state of civilization and those who are at the outset of the use of their native intelligence'. Dufour enobles the islanders in his use of stately Olympian postures and classical garb; the women seem to be clothed in fashionable Empire gowns.

The work occupies an important place in the history of wallpaper as the first successful scenic paper, following an anonymous street scene of *circa* 1797 and Jean Zuber's *Vues de Suisse* of 1804. Up to the 1860s more than a hundred scenic wallpapers were produced. They had antecedents in painted Chinese papers, but were also partly inspired by panoramas; two panoramas were open to the Paris public at the turn of the century. The scenic paper went beyond traditional wallpaper in several ways. It dispensed with the 'repeating' design and the idea of wallpaper as a substitute or imitation of some other material. At the same time, by disregarding the restraint of the wall, wallpaper could become more pictorially complex and the imagination of its designers less fettered. Following the example of Charvet, manufacturers roamed widely through the classics, history, literature, current events, geography and topography for suitable subjects.

In a variety of ways this beautiful wallpaper is a measure of taste in Napoleonic France.

A Gothic allegorical tapestry depicting scenes from the *Roman de la Rose*, Tournai, 1460–65,
13ft 9in by 15ft 3in (419cm by 465cm)
London £187,000 ($299,200). 11.III.83

The *Roman de la Rose*, a highly popular allegorical poem in the Middle Ages, was written in two parts
during the thirteenth century: the first part, which has been described as 'an artistic presentment of
the love philosophy of the troubadours', was composed by Guillaume de Lorris, *circa* 1235. The longer
and more didactic conclusion was written *circa* 1275 by Jean de Meung. This tapestry shows *L'amant*
seeking admission to the Castle of the Rose, surrounded by allegorical figures, including *Courtoisie*,
Bel Accueil, *Honte*, *Dangier*, *Paour*, *Jalousie* and the blindfolded *Dieu d'amours*.

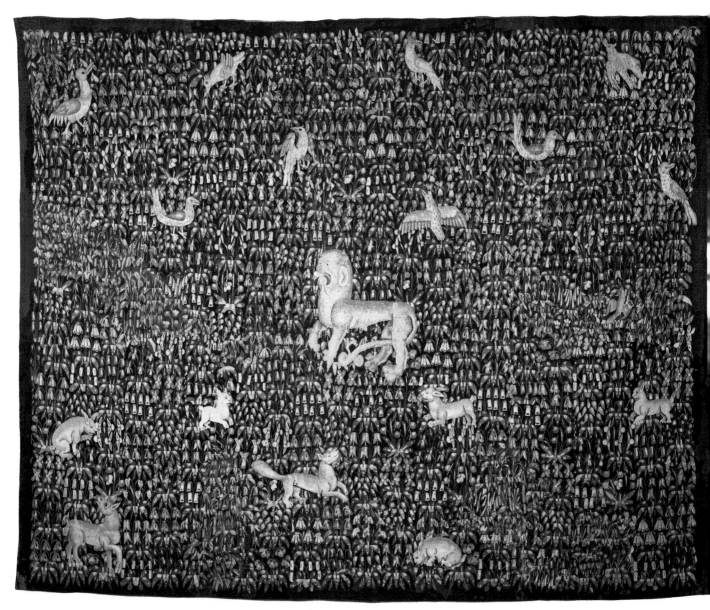

A Franco-Flemish *millefleurs* tapestry, probably Tournai, *circa* 1500
8ft 4in by 10ft 4in (254cm by 315cm)
New York $132,000 (£82,500). 3.XII.82

A Louis XV Gobelins tapestry, *Dom Quixotte estant a Barcelonne danse au bal que luy donne Dom Antonio*,
by Pierre-François Cozette after Charles Coypel, signed and dated *1758*,
12ft by 15ft 5in (365cm by 470cm)
Monte Carlo FF1,054,500 (£87,293: $139,669). 26.VI.83

Charles Coypel designed twenty-eight tapestry cartoons with scenes from *Don Quixote*, which were
woven with a variety of decorative borders by the Gobelins factory until the Revolution. This tapestry
remained at the factory during the Revolution and was given by Napoleon to the Prince of Hesse-
Darmstadt in 1810.

Silver

A Charles II silver-gilt tankard, presented to Captain Hugh Piper by George Monck, 1st Duke of
Albemarle, maker's mark of Francis Leake, London, 1675, height $8\frac{1}{4}$in (21cm)
London £85,800 ($137,280). 13.VI.83
From the collection of Sir John Vyvyan, Bt

A set of twenty-four Queen Anne silver-gilt dinner plates, maker's mark of John Gibbons, London, 1703, diameter $9\frac{1}{2}$in (24.2cm)
London £169,400 ($271,040). 13.VI.83

These plates are almost certainly part of a set ordered by John Methuen upon his appointment as Ambassador Extraordinary to Portugal in 1703, and bear his arms. The same year he concluded the 'Methuen Treaty' in which the King of Portugal allowed the import of English woollen goods in return for favourable terms for Portuguese wines, with the result that Port gradually superseded Burgundy as England's most popular wine.

A pair of George II condiment boxes, bearing the arms of Sir William Irby, Bt, maker's mark of Edward Wakelin, London, 1749, width of each $4\frac{1}{2}$in (11.6cm)
London £25,300 ($40,480). 13.VI.83

A set of three Queen Anne silver-gilt casters, maker's mark of Philip Rollos I, London, *circa* 1705, height 10¼in and 8¼in (26cm and 21cm)
London £96,800 ($154,880). 13.VI.83

Philip Rollos I held the position of Subordinate Goldsmith to William III and Queen Anne.

A Queen Anne silver-gilt ewer and basin, maker's mark of David Willaume I, London, 1702, height of ewer 9½in (24.1cm), width of basin 15¾in (40cm)
New York $137,500 (£85,938). 21.IV.83
Formerly in the collection of the Duke of Cumberland

The ewer and basin bear the royal arms of Queen Anne before the Union with Scotland. Mrs Abigail Masham, Woman of the Bedchamber to Queen Anne, describes the use of such pieces in her account of the queen's toilet: 'When the Queen washed her hands, the page of the backstairs brought and set down upon a side table the basin and ewer. Then the bedchamber woman set it before the Queen and knelt on the other side of the table over against the Queen, the bedchamber lady only looking on. The bedchamber woman poured the water out of the ewer upon the Queen's hands.' As well as several related pieces by this maker, there are two similar ewers bearing the royal arms, one by Philip Rollos I, marked for 1705 (sold at Sotheby's in London on 27 June 1963, and now in the Victoria and Albert Museum, London), and the other by Philip Rollos II, marked for 1717.

The Bristol ewer and basin

Elaine Barr

One of the most original and historically important pieces of early English Rococo silver was auctioned last June (Fig. 1). The silver-gilt ewer and basin were made in 1735/36 by George Wickes, goldsmith to Frederick, Prince of Wales. Wickes has long been recognized as one of the great masters of the first half of the eighteenth century, but the Bristol pieces present a new dimension – the revelation of an early date for the importation of French Rococo prints into England.

Rarely have the origins of such objects been so well documented. The ewer and basin are recorded in Wickes's *Gentlemen's* [clients'] *Ledger* on 15 January 1735/36 (Fig. 2). Wickes, departing from his usual laconic style, described them as 'a fine Bason [*sic*] and Ewer'. They were made apparently for Leonell Lyde Esquire, Mayor of Bristol. It has, however, recently been discovered that Lyde was acting for the Common Council of the Corporation of Bristol, and that the pieces were destined to mark the retirement of John Scrope, the city's Recorder since 1728.

As Secretary to the Treasury, Scrope had served the wider interests of Bristol, notably in opposing the African Society's attempts to monopolize the slave trade. In lieu of his Recorder's salary, 'which he declined to accept', the Common Council on 6 August 1735 unanimously voted him 'a present of a piece of Plate to the value of one hundred Guineas'.[1] It was duly commissioned from Wickes – scrupulously referred to throughout as 'Mr Wickes' – and, in Scrope's own words, 'the most curious Bason and Ewer that ever was seen' were delivered to him on 23 February 1735/36.[2] Scrope and Wickes were no strangers: already in 1732 the goldsmith had made him an épergne, an earlier gift from the Common Council.[3] Wickes's bill for the piece, together with his receipt for payment of the 1736 commission, is preserved in the Bristol Record Office.

The ewer and basin left his workshop ungilded, but Wickes's ledger account for Francis Fane, Scrope's nephew–heir, records on 27 March 1736 'doing up *the* Bason and pott [*sic*] as New & Coulering and Guilding'. Scrope's own account was debited with '2 Cases for *ye* Bason and Ewer', followed by 'To Eight [pence] per oz on *the* Bason & Ewer . . . £9 3s 4d'. Both charges were later waived, 'charged by mistake'. When the pieces were returned for burnishing in June 1741, Wickes noted, 'This account allow'd to ballance. G.W.'. Two weeks later the then considerable sum of £40 was credited to Scrope, 'By Cash allowed per G.W.'.

Fig. 1
A George II silver-gilt ewer and basin, maker's mark of George Wickes, London, 1735, height of
ewer 14¼in (36.2cm), diameter of basin 21¾in (55.2cm)
London £176,000 ($281,600). 13.VI.83

Fig. 2
Detail of the entry in
Wickes's *Gentlemen's Ledger*,
15 January 1735/36
Reproduced courtesy of
Garrard & Co. Ltd, London

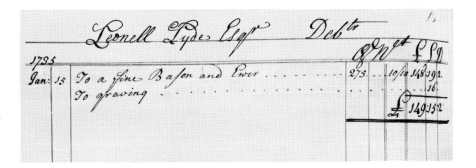

Fig. 3
Detail of the left-hand cartouche on the basin

Fig. 4
JACQUES DE LA JOUE
Second Livre de Cartouches, p.10, engraved by
Gabriel Huquier
Reproduced courtesy of the Victoria and Albert
Museum, London

This quasi-intimacy can only be explained in the light of the family connections of Wickes's wife, Alder. Her mother was born Aldworth, a member of a Bristol family of merchant princes. Scropes appear in several Aldworth documents: the Thomas Scrope named in a Feet of Fines in 1681 was almost certainly the father of John.

John Scrope's nephews, Thomas, Francis and Henry Fane, were all life-long clients of Wickes. Thomas, an eminent Bristol lawyer, was Clerk to the Merchant Adventurers. He must, however, have been acting for the Sheriffs of Bristol when in 1740, 1741 and 1742 he ordered from Wickes silver-gilt scabbards for the State Sword. He succeeded to the earldom of Westmorland in 1762. Francis, a barrister-at-law, was Scrope's heir. Their close ties are reflected in Wickes's ledgers: £24 10s incurred by Francis for flatware and a coffee pot was transferred to the account of his indulgent uncle. The Fanes' brother-in-law, Dr Creswick, Dean of Bath and Wells, also patronized Wickes, in company with many other Bristol dignitaries.

After 1741 the ewer and basin vanish from the ledgers. They were no doubt familiar to Scrope's friends, including Sir Robert Walpole (himself a client of Wickes). His son, Horace Walpole, left a vivid word picture of Scrope, 'a most testy little old gentleman', who in 1733 tweaked the nose of Alderman Micaiah Perry in the House of Commons and would have fought a duel with him over the Excise Bill. Scrope, who 'had been in Monmouth's Rebellion when very young, and carried intelligence to Holland in woman's clothes', was still a match for Walpole's enemies in 1742. He refused to take the Secret Committee oath, saying 'that he was fourscore years old and did not care whether he spent the few months he had to live in the Tower or not'.

Scrope lived until 21 April 1752. By his will,[4] his family estate at Wormsley, Oxfordshire, with the 'rest and residue . . . of what nature or kind soever', passed to Francis Fane who presumably inherited the ewer and basin. In 1756 Francis died leaving the Scrope estate to his brother Henry, with the 'plate . . . which shall be in or belonging to my house at Wormsley'.[5] There is no mention of plate in Henry's rambling will of 1777.[6] His West Country estates went to his son Francis, the rest 'both real and personal' to his son John, who must thus have acquired Wormsley and the Bristol pieces. John died in 1824 and all his plate, unitemized, was bequeathed to his wife, Lady Elizabeth Fane.[7]

By the 1770s the Rococo was outmoded and, in their pursuit of Neoclassicism, the clients of Wickes's old firm (now John Wakelin and William Tayler) handed in large quantities of 'old fashioned' plate for melting down and remaking. John Fane was no exception. He had already traded in 302 oz of 'Sundry Old Plate' in 1774 and, in 1778, a year after his father's death, another 959 oz 'as per Waste Book'. That horrific record has unfortunately not survived and, although such old plate was sometimes itemized, it was not listed in John Fane's account on either occasion. His patronage of the firm ceased abruptly in 1790.

A search of all clients' accounts in the ledgers from 1774 to 1790 failed to disclose the ewer and basin. Somehow they survived the melting pot and the passage of time to surface in 1876 as the Doncaster Racing Cup, supplied by Wickes's nineteenth-century successors, R. & S. Garrard & Co. They could not have foreseen the interest their founder's design would create a century later.

The applied cast and chased decoration on the basin is a very early manifestation of full-blown Rococo, which could only have been achieved by someone in touch with French trends. Michael Snodin of the Victoria and Albert Museum has drawn attention to the influence of Jacques de la Joue. The design of the left-hand cartouche (Fig. 3) follows closely one published in his *Second Livre de Cartouches* (Fig. 4), engraved by Gabriel Huquier. The Rococo details that frame the profiles also owe much to this source, which was published in Paris probably about 1734.

The ewer is remarkable for its shape – not even Paul de Lamerie had arrived at this form in 1736. Water and wine are represented by bulrushes and vines, suggesting the vessel's dual purpose. The Berainesque mask (perhaps Poseidon, Dionysus or a river god, possibly Tiber) and the eagle (a link with the Caesars) consort curiously with the plethora of Rococo detail. The female head on the handle, which may well have been intended as a likeness of Britannia and Patriotism, is of particular interest (Fig. 5). In the Yale Center for British Art, in a collection convincingly attributed to the designer and chaser Augustin Heckel, there is an unsigned drawing of a female head with a similar collar. Heckel, who was working in London in the 1730s, would have been familiar with the decorative designs of Watteau, whose detached heads wear these distinctive collars; they do not seem to occur in other contemporary engravings.

Fig. 5
Detail of the handle of the ewer, showing the female
head, probably a likeness of Britannia or Patriotism

The decorative motifs appear to have been carefully chosen, possibly in consultation with Scrope or Francis Fane. The general theme is *gravitas*, symbolized by the classical heads of the twelve Caesars on the basin: the Caesars would have appealed to Scrope, the lawyer, who owed his courtesy title of baron to a judicial appointment which he held until 1724. The wealth of Bristol depended largely on the sea, hence the cascades of water, shells, fish scales and marine festoons. Peace and Victory, in the form of palms and laurel leaves, may refer to Scrope's youthful military exploits, whilst the cornucopia signifies Plenty. It fell to Wickes to devise a design that would encompass all the aspects of Scrope's career and to place them in a Rococo setting, which must have been very avant-garde in 1735.

The growing interest in the Rococo period is not confined to the art historian and this is reflected in the Victoria and Albert Museum's decision to stage a major exhibition in 1984. The exhibition 'Rococo: Art and Design in Hogarth's England', will run from 16 May to 30 September and will be devoted to all aspects of the style.

I am grateful to Mary Williams, the City Archivist of Bristol, John Culme of Sotheby's and Michael Snodin of the Victoria and Albert Museum, London, for their generous help in the preparation of this article.

NOTES
1. City of Bristol, Proceedings of the Common Council, 6 August 1735
2. City of Bristol, Proceedings of the Common Council, 4 March 1735/36
3. City of Bristol, Proceedings of the Common Council, 5 January 1731/32
4. P.R.O., P.C.C. Prob 11/794 Bettesworth
5. P.R.O., P.C.C. Prob 11/831 Herring
6. P.R.O., P.C.C. Prob 11/1032 Collier
7. P.R.O., P.C.C. Prob 11/1685 Erskine

A George II soup tureen and cover, maker's mark of Paul de Lamerie, London, 1741,
width 17¾in (45.1cm)
London £74,800 ($119,680). 11.XI.82

A pair of George IV silver-gilt ewers, maker's mark of Edward Farrell, London, 1824,
height of each 23¼in (59cm)
New York $110,000 (£68,750). 17.XII.82

These ewers were bought by the Duke of York from Kensington Lewis, a successful entrepreneur and
dealer, who employed Farrell between about 1816 and 1834. The influence of sixteenth and
seventeenth-century pieces on Farrell's style, demonstrated here, is perhaps explained by Lewis's
taste for plate of that period. The bases bear the royal arms of France, suggesting that the ewers were
intended as a gift to Charles X on his coronation, which took place on 29 May 1825.

Opposite
A Hanukah lamp, maker's mark of George Wilhelm Margraff, Berlin, *circa* 1776, height 26in (66cm)
New York $110,000 (£68,750). 23.VI.83

A fourteenth-century double cup

Timothy Husband

The appearance of three hitherto unknown pieces of fourteenth-century silver (Fig. 1), offered at auction last March, ranks as one of the most important discoveries of medieval secular silver in the last hundred years. The finest of these objects was a *Doppelkopf* or 'double cup' (Fig. 2). It is in remarkably good condition and, beyond the pitted surface expected of plate that has been buried, it is largely intact. It comprises two finely balanced sections of similar form and profile; the upper cup serves as a cover when placed over the lower half. On the interior of the lower section is an applied enamelled print with a helm crested by three up-ended Jewish hats, reserved in silver against a red enamel background (Fig. 3). The finial is inset with an escutcheon bearing three Jewish hats, also reserved in silver and against the remnants of a red background (Fig. 4).

The form of the escutcheon and the character of the heraldic devices are consistent with heraldic configurations of the first half of the fourteenth century, sharing affinities with devices represented in the *Manessische Handschrift* and the *Züricher Wappenrolle*. The employment of a helm on the interior medallion suggests a family coat of arms, while the reduced arrangement of the Jews' hats on the exterior escutcheon may indicate a more general device. Neither has been identified, but a Jewish context is certainly suggested.

The double cup was a particular type of Germanic vessel, which had achieved its developed form by the end of the thirteenth century and endured without fundamental change throughout the next four centuries. Depicted in virtually all media, double cups are seen on the tables of great princes and minor burghers, in guild and civic halls, as well as on the sideboards of middle-class merchants. St Eloi is frequently depicted working a double cup, while in representations of the Adoration, one of the Three Kings is invariably shown presenting the Christ Child with a double cup overflowing with precious spices or gold coins. From documents we know that emperors, kings and princely lords emulated the latter practice in their exchanges of state gifts. The importance placed on double cups throughout the German-speaking medieval world was not due to their function as drinking vessels, for in this regard they were remarkably ungainly, particularly the more elaborate later medieval forms. Rather, their importance derived from the surrounding customs and rituals they served, and the amuletic and supernatural powers invested in them.

Fig. 1
Back, left to right
A parcel-gilt flagon, early fourteenth century, height 13¾in (35cm). £60,500 ($96,800)
A parcel-gilt ewer, early fourteenth century, height 12⅝in (32cm). £23,100 ($36,960)
Front
A parcel-gilt double cup, early fourteenth century, diameter 4⅛in (10.6cm). £132,000 ($211,200)

These pieces of silver were sold in London on 7 March 1983; the double cup is now in The Cloisters, Metropolitan Museum of Art, New York

Double cups were essentially the apparatus of the age-old custom of *Minnetrinken*, love or devotional toasts to the Goddess Minne. Because of their pagan origins, such practices were continually proscribed by the Church Fathers, but, as in many such instances, levelled *dicta* could not curb entrenched custom. By the fourteenth century, *Minnetrinken* in a Christian context were widespread. Perhaps the *Minnetrinken* most tacitly sanctioned by the Church, and therefore the most ubiquitous, were the *Johannesminne* in honour of the Evangelist, invoked not on a specific day but in times of particular need. The Three Kings, whose relics, venerated in Cologne, inspired one of the more popular high Gothic cults, were also the objects of *Minnetrinken*. It is in this context that the present double cup must be understood. A band encircling the upper vessel is boldly inscribed with the names of the Three Kings: *CASPAR + MELCHIOR + WALTAZAR +*.

The heraldic devices, which suggest a Jewish context for this double cup, would seem to present something of a contradiction. There is, however, a possible explanation that reconciles the apparent contradiction, and adds an exceptional, if somewhat speculative, dimension to this object.

Epiphany was thought to mark the true New Year, and Epiphany eve was considered a magical night. Animals could talk, and any sight of celestial conjunctions in threes granted the viewer three wishes. In every region, particular types of bread were baked, distributed and eaten for good luck. On Three Kings' day, the future could be foretold by such means as interpreting the forms made by drops of molten lead as they hit cold water, and the Three Kings brought protection against a litany of complaints, diseases and evils. All these superstitions and practices had little relevance to religious celebration. In this context, the inscription on the double cup might be interpreted as a purely talismanic or amuletic reinforcement to the *Minnetrinken*, which could be widely indulged by all, including Jews.

During the fourteenth century under the Luxemburg king–emperors, the Jews in Germany and Bohemia, with the catastrophic exception of the 1349 pogroms, enjoyed relatively protected and prosperous times. The monied classes experienced rapid enhancement of position in a burgeoning monetary system eager for credit to fuel an expanding economy. Since the time of Emperor Frederick II, the Jews in Germany had been explicitly designated *Kammerknechte* and were nominally under imperial protection. In lands where Charles IV was prince by title, he took practical steps to draw the Jews under his protection. In 1338, as Margrave of Moravia, for example, he forbade the citizens of Neupilsen to cause injury to the Jews of that city by either word or deed. In this climate, many Jews were able to amass great wealth and to rise to prominence as imperial financiers, court advisers and high-ranking bureaucrats. The names of the most powerful Jews in Prague, such as Lazar, Man and Trostlin, appear frequently in the records and accounts of Charles IV.

In 1351, Charles IV, in whose lands and during whose lifetime this double cup was assuredly executed, invited all the Jews of Bohemia to Prague to celebrate the marriage of Lazar, the foremost Jewish capitalist of that imperial city. One is strongly tempted to associate the present double cup with such a celebration.

A set of five nested silver beakers of hexagonal cross section, now in the Germanisches Nationalmuseum, Nuremberg, provides important evidence for establishing a more

Fig. 2
The double cup, showing the ring handle, the gilt band engraved with the names of the Three Kings,
and the heater-shaped shield on the finial

Fig. 3
Detail of the print inside the lower section,
bearing a helm crested by three up-ended
Jewish hats, originally against a red enamel
ground

Fig. 4
Detail of the shield on the finial, bearing three
Jewish hats set centrifugally, originally against
a red enamel ground

Fig. 6
View of one beaker from above,
showing the escutcheon of three
Jewish hats set centrifugally
attached to its base
Reproduced courtesy of the
Germanisches Nationalmuseum,
Nuremberg

Fig. 5
A nest of five silver beakers, Prague, *circa* 1310–35,
height of largest beaker $3\frac{3}{8}$ in (9.2cm)
Reproduced courtesy of the Germanisches Nationalmuseum, Nuremberg

specific framework for the double cup (Fig. 5). Attached to the interior base of each of
these graduated interfacing beakers is an escutcheon similar in form to that on the
double cup. The devices, all reserved in silver against a cross-hatched silver ground,
consist of, in descending order: the *Bindenschild* of Austria, the white eagle of Poland,
the double-tailed lion of Bohemia, three centrifugally arranged Jews' hats as in the
present example (Fig. 6), and a rampant wolf *à dexter* with a later Hebrew inscription
incised above. Previous attempts to decipher this heraldic assemblage have sought
out an individual who would bring the three royal houses into conjunction, yielding
two possibilities: Elizabeth (1292–1330), daughter of King Wenzel II of Bohemia and
Poland; and Rixa Elizabeth (1288–1335), heiress to the Polish kingdom after the death
of her father, Przemyslav II, in 1296. This interpretation implies a date prior to 1335,
which is consistent with the style of the beakers, but does not account for two of the
heraldic devices.

   The presence of a Jewish device among those of three royal houses might be explained if it were read as the device of an association or fraternity of high-ranking
Jews who were in the protection and service of the houses represented. The owner of
the Nuremberg beakers was probably attached to Charles IV's court, as they were
excavated at Kuttenberg, east of Prague, the location of a favourite imperial residence.

The exact correspondence of the heraldic device of three Jews' hats arranged centrifugally brings the present double cup into close connection with the beakers in Nuremberg. The objects are nearly, if not exactly, contemporaneous, so the interpretation of the Nuremberg device may also help to explain that on the double cup.

It is difficult to locate the manufacture of the double cup. There are a number of silver double cups, all dating from the first half of the fourteenth century, that may be assembled in a single group of close stylistic affinity. They are at distinct variance with the present example; none are particularly spheroid in shape, rather they are deeply compressed at the joining, creating an entirely different proportional aesthetic. The cups were excavated over a broad area extending from Switzerland, through the upper Rhineland and the Bodensee, into Swabia and the middle Rhineland. Given the wide geographic distribution, it is less probable that they were produced in a single or associated workshops than that they represent a conventional type which pervaded the metalwork production of the region as a whole. It seems unlikely, therefore, that the present double cup, born of a very different aesthetic, could have been produced in the same region. So one is tempted to seek its origins in the more easterly reaches of the Luxemburg–Wittelsbach–Habsburg domains, most probably in upper Bavaria or Bohemia.

Although the double cup was certainly excavated, nothing is known about the find. However, a silver trove that relates to this piece was unearthed in 1969 at Lingenfeld, a small town near Speyer. Buried in an earthenware jug were a number of silver objects, including a double cup of upper Rhenish origin, and 2,369 coins all dateable prior to 1350, thereby providing an indication of the date of the silver, as well as suggesting an historical context for the hoard.

In 1347, the Black Death broke out in southern Europe, and by late 1348 had spread north of the Alps and deep into the German territories. The deadly onslaught brought about mass fear of the most profound sort. Scapegoats were sought, and the Jews became the immediate target. Blamed for causing the plague, the Jews throughout Europe became the object of a massive and virulent pogrom. On 10 and 25 January 1349, a flurry of anti-Semitic decrees and confiscations were executed in Speyer. By March, killings had begun in earnest. In this context, there seems little doubt that the Lingenfeld treasure was hoarded by a wealthy and panicked Jew early in that desperate year. Given the device on the double cup, it is tempting to speculate that this precious object, along with the other two vessels purportedly found with it, owes its survival to a similar circumstance.

The double cup appears to be the only known example of its type and one of the very few extant examples of early fourteenth-century German secular plate. By its apparent use in the context of *Minnetrinken*, it vividly reflects medieval folkloric belief, celebratory ritual and everyday custom. As the heraldic devices strongly suggest a Jewish context, this double cup may be numbered among a mere handful of high Gothic objects that document an aspect of Jewish life in medieval Christian Europe. On the basis of the identical heraldic devices, a close association with the Kuttenberg beakers seems highly probable. We are then able to place this vessel in an historical context documenting the role of Jews in the imperial court at Prague. As such, it becomes an object of considerable historical significance.

A standing salt, Middelburg, 1622, height 6¼in (16cm)
Amsterdam DFl 67,280 (£14,852:$23,763). 16.III.83

Opposite
A silver-gilt teapot, maker's mark of Matthäus Baur II, Augsburg, *circa* 1690, height 6⅞in (17.5cm)
Geneva SFr 198,000 (£59,104:$94,566). 12.V.83

The style of this teapot closely resembles contemporary Chinese porcelain examples. It is engraved with mounted warriors and with portraits of Ottoman emperors after engravings by Theodor de Bry (see black and white illustrations). This perhaps suggests that it was made to commemorate the victory of the Imperial army over the Turks after the Siege of Vienna in 1683.

A silver-gilt soup tureen with cover and stand, maker's mark of Jean-Baptiste-Claude Odiot, Paris, 1819, width 19½ in (49.6cm)
Geneva SFr 577,500 (£172,388 : $275,821). 30.XI.82

This soup tureen is one of a pair from a large service made for the Polish general, Count François Xavier Branicki and his wife, Alexandra Vassilievna Engelhardt, the illegitimate daughter of Grigory Potemkin and Catherine the Great of Russia. The original invoice and designs remain in the archives of La Maison Odiot in Paris, and reveal that the total cost for the pair of tureens was about 17,200 francs. Many pieces of this service, including the other tureen, are now in the Rijksmuseum, Amsterdam.

Opposite
Six silver-gilt candlesticks originally part of a larger set, maker's mark of Christian Heinrich Ingermann, Dresden, *circa* 1750, height of each 9⅝ in (24.5cm)
Geneva SFr 385,000 (£114,925 : $183,880). 12.V.83

These candlesticks are engraved with the cypher of Augustus III (1733–63), Duke of Saxony and King of Poland, who is known to have supplemented the great silver collection of his father, Augustus the Strong.

European ceramics

An Urbino dish with a scene from the Battle of Mühlberg (24 April 1547), after an engraving by Aeneo Vico, inscribed on the reverse *La Presa del' Duca de Sasonia, circa* 1555–60, diameter $17\frac{3}{4}$in (45cm)
London £16,500 ($26,400). 26.IV.83
From the collection of the Lord Astor of Hever

A Florentine 'oak leaf' jar, mid-fifteenth century, height $7\frac{5}{8}$ in (19.3cm)
New York $35,200 (£22,000). 3.XII.82

From left to right
An albarello, inscribed *GIRCILIO*, Neapolitan or Tuscan, late fifteenth century,
height 11¾in (30cm). London £8,800 ($14,080). 26.IV.83
An albarello, bearing the arms of the Duke of Calabria, Neapolitan or Tuscan,
late fifteenth century, height 12in (30.5cm). London £9,900 ($15,840). 26.IV.83
An albarello, inscribed *SANCZONE*, Neapolitan or Tuscan, late fifteenth century,
height 11¾in (30cm). London £9,350 ($14,960). 26.IV.83
These albarelli were made for the Aragonese Pharmacy at the Castel Nuovo, Naples.

A Castel Durante dish painted in the manner of Nicola da Urbino, *circa* 1525–28,
diameter 6⅞in (17.5cm)
London £10,450 ($16,720). 26.IV.83

A Nuremberg documentary faïence tankard with contemporary
pewter mounts, painted by Georg Friedrich Grebner, signed
and dated 23 June 1730, height $10\frac{7}{8}$in (27.5cm)
London £19,250 ($30,800). 26.IV.83

This tankard was made to commemorate the 200th anniversary
of the Confession of Augsburg, the most important statement of
Protestant belief made during the Reformation.

A Creussen stoneware tankard with contemporary
pewter mounts, from the workshop of the
Vest family, early seventeenth century,
height $7\frac{7}{8}$in (20cm)
London £7,480 ($11,968). 26.IV.83

A Fürstenberg vase painted by Johann Heinrich Christian Eli, marked *A.K.* in underglaze-blue
and incised *AK/St, circa* 1830, height 14½in (37cm)
London £5,720 ($9,152). 15.III.83

A Sèvres tea service painted with Egyptian scenes by Nicholas-Antoine Le Bel, marked *M. Imple. de Sèvres*, *8DV* and *8j*, November–December 1808
Monte Carlo FF 444,000 (£36,755:$58,808). 25.VI.83

This is the second of four Egyptian-taste services made at Sèvres. It belonged to the Empress Josephine and was probably presented to her by Napoleon in December 1808 as a New Year present. The painted scenes are taken from Vivant Denon's *Voyage dans la Basse et la Haute Egypte* (1802).

A pair of gilt-bronze-mounted Meissen figures of Indian ring-necked parakeets modelled by
Johann Joachim Kaendler, the mounts marked with crowned C, *circa* 1741,
total height of each 13in (33cm); 13⅞in (35.2cm)
New York $61,600 (£38,500). 7.V.83

A delftware 'royal portrait' plate,
inscribed *G R III*, probably Lambeth,
circa 1761, diameter 8¾in (22.2cm)
London £3,960 ($6,336). 1.III.83
From the collection of the late Louis L. Lipski

This plate was probably made to commemorate
the marriage of George III and Queen Charlotte
in 1761.

A delftware vase, probably Bristol,
mid-eighteenth century,
height 6½in (16.5cm)
London £1,870 ($2,992). 1.III.83
From the collection of the late
Louis L. Lipski

A Worcester blue and white mustard pot, marked with incised cross and a cross in underglaze-blue, *circa* 1754, height 4in (10.1cm)
London £3,520 ($5,632). 17.XII.82

A Chelsea rabbit tureen and cover, marked with red anchor, *circa* 1755, length 14½in (36.8cm)
London £9,900 ($15,840). 15.III.83

Opposite
Above A Bristol documentary sauce boat, marked with embossed *Bristoll* overpainted with a green leaf
and incised *P*, *circa* 1750–51, length 7⅝in (19.3cm)
London £7,700 ($12,320). 12.VII.83
Below A Bristol documentary sauce boat, marked with embossed *Bristoll* overpainted with a green leaf
and incised *R*, *circa* 1750–51, length 7⅝in (19.3cm)
London £8,250 ($13,200). 12.VII.83

The Swall Collection of nineteenth-century continental porcelain

Barbara E. Deisroth

The impressive collection of nineteenth-century European ceramics formed by the late Wilfred Swall was the most important of its kind ever to have appeared at auction. The three sessions totalled over $2,600,000, the first sale alone making $1,074,370. The lavish and grandiose have always been aspects of American interior design and it is no great surprise to find that the collection, with its wealth of elaborate and monumental porcelains, was amassed entirely in North America.

Wilfred Swall, a Californian plum farmer, began his collection in 1952 and added constantly to it until his death in July 1982. In fact, the last purchase arrived some days after he had died. The 1,500 or so pieces were housed in a very small dilapidated barn, whose modest exterior belied the opulence of the contents. Inside, the two rooms were fitted with tiers of platforms to hold an array of impressive vases, columns and pedestals. Above, the walls were covered with painted plates, whilst recent acquisitions lay on the floor in the centre of each room. Some smaller objects were kept carefully in cabinets, and additional sets of portrait plates were stored in discarded paint cans.

Mr Swall's taste was varied and apparently insatiable, but his eye for quality was unerring. This was reflected in the exceptional prices attained for the finest pieces in the three sales. Among the most notable bids were those of $121,000 for a pair of 'Vienna' vases painted by Kreysa with mythological scenes (Fig. 1), and $63,250 for a meticulously executed plaque by A. Knÿe, showing a lavish interior with odalisques (Fig. 2); this was the highest price ever paid for a Berlin plaque. A massive and important pair of Russian vases fetched $68,200 (Fig. 3). These had been decorated by Alexander Petrovich Nesterov, a master at the St Petersburg Imperial factory, with figures in the French style after Nicolas Lancret. Almost as surprising was the price of $35,200 for a Minton maiolica 'Prometheus' vase, so called after the moulded figure of the hero on the cover. Around the body runs a lively frieze of hunting scenes, involving a lion and a hippopotamus.

In a field where the quality of decoration more often than not falls well below standard, the collection exhibited only examples of the highest quality and of exceptional size. Not only did the sales prove a great success, more than doubling the most optimistic estimates, but they added greatly to the interest in European ceramics of the nineteenth century.

Fig. 1
A pair of 'Vienna' vases and covers, painted by Kreysa, indistinctly signed, each marked with blue
shields, late nineteenth century, height of each 5ft 7in (170cm)
New York $121,000 (£75,625). 18.VI.83
From the collection of the late Wilfred Swall

Fig. 2
A Berlin plaque, painted by A. Knÿe, signed, marked with impressed sceptre and *K.P.M.*,
late nineteenth century, length 36in (91.4cm)
New York $63,250 (£39,531). 5.II.83
From the collection of the late Wilfred Swall

Fig. 3
A pair of St Petersburg Imperial vases, painted by Alexander Nesterov after Nicolas Lancret,
each signed and dated *1849*, height of each 4ft 9½in (146cm)
New York $68,200 (£42,625). 5.II.83
From the collection of the late Wilfred Swall

George Owen's pierced wares

Michael R. Turner

The intricate work of George Owen, employed at the Royal Worcester porcelain factory for over fifty-five years until his death in 1917, was well represented by the cabinet objects sold last February (see opposite). These fragile and meticulously pierced pieces display the astonishing skill of a craftsman whose achievement has been increasingly appreciated in the last few years. While both Royal Worcester and the nearby Grainger and Co. produced reticulated wares during the later part of the nineteenth century, Owen developed the craft to almost unbelievable perfection.

The process of piercing was difficult and time consuming. The clay body of the object had to be kept at just the right state of 'leather' hardness; if too moist, the body would collapse; if too dry, the pressure needed for the knife to cut would depress the side of the vessel. There were numerous other production problems. The finely potted body, often especially cast by George's son, was prone to warp in the kiln, and the slightest flaw in the clay could cause a vase to explode during any one of the three or four firings.

Owen maintained that he never used any mechanical aids and that the evenly spaced perforations, often in graduated sizes, were produced solely by the judgement of his eyes. It is difficult to ascertain whether this is true: he worked in secret and alone; visitors were required to wait outside until he had put away his tools and placed the object on which he was working to one side. However, he was ambidextrous and able to use the small knives and saws with equal pressure from left or right. This may, in part, account for the uniformity of execution that is typical of his work. It is also thought that he dipped the piercing instruments in oil, so that the tiny pieces of cut-out clay would not fall into the vessel, where they might be difficult to remove.

It is tempting to count the number of holes that make up the lace-like pattern of honeycomb and formal borders. One example of Owen's skill, a vase 7in high, sold at Sotheby's Belgravia in January 1972, had a pencilled note on the base stating that there were 2,034 perforations in the body. A more elaborate piece, exhibited at the Chicago Exhibition in 1893, was said to have over 5,000 apertures.

Other workmen at the factory attempted reticulation, but their results seem clumsy compared to the work of the master. Their pieces are unsigned, whereas most of Owen's examples bear an incised or gilt signature on the base, sometimes with the date of production. In the history of European ceramics there is no comparable artist and his signed works are now purchased for collections all over the world.

A photograph of George Owen in his workshop

From left to right
A vase and cover pierced by George Owen, marked with printed gilt crowned circle, incised signature and date code for 1919, height 9½in (24.1cm). £3,960($6,336)
A court shoe pierced by George Owen, marked with printed gilt crowned circle, incised signature and date code for 1917, length 6¼in (15.8cm). £3,850($6,160)
A vase and cover pierced by George Owen, marked with printed gilt crowned circle, incised signature and date code for 1910, height 12¾in (32.4cm). £4,180($6,688)
A casket and cover pierced by George Owen, marked with printed gilt crowned circle, incised signature and date code for 1918, length 6¼in (15.8cm). £3,080($4,928)
A vase and cover pierced by George Owen, marked with printed gilt crowned circle, incised signature and date code for 1918, height 9in (22.8cm). £3,960($6,336)

The Royal Worcester porcelain illustrated above was sold in London on 22 February 1983.

Glass

Right
A transparent-enamelled beaker by Samuel Mohn,
Dresden, *circa* 1810, height 3⅞in (10cm)
London £4,840 ($7,744). 15.XI.82
From the collection of Mr and Mrs Helfried Krug

Below, left
A Venetian enamelled and gilt armorial pilgrim flask,
circa 1492, height 14in (35.5cm)
London £8,800 ($14,080). 18.VII.83

The arms are those of Bentivoglio and the flask was
probably made in connection with the marriage of
Alessandro Bentivoglio and Ippolita Sforza in 1492.

Below, right
A Beilby enamelled ale glass, *circa* 1770, height 7¼in (18.5cm)
London £4,180 ($6,688). 18.VII.83

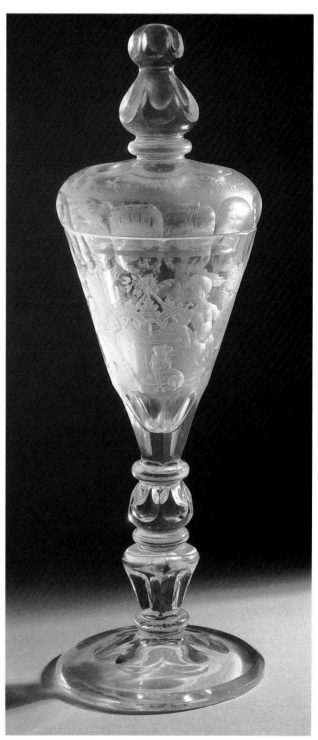

An enamelled and gilt armorial *Stangenglas*, South German or Venetian, dated *1556*, height 11⅛in (28.3cm) London £8,800 ($14,080). 1.XI.82

The arms are those of Ortenburg and Spaur of Pflaum.

A goblet and cover attributed to the Master HI, inscribed *CAROLV.XI.REX.Svec*, Potsdam, *circa* 1695, height 16¾in (42.5cm) London £8,800 ($14,080). 14.III.83 From the collection of Mr and Mrs Helfried Krug

Art Nouveau and Art Deco

An ebonized wood side table designed by Philip Webb, 1860s, length 60in (152.5cm)
London £19,250 ($30,800). 28.IV.83

This table belonged to Vernon Lushington, an early patron of the Pre-Raphaelite circle, particularly
Morris, Webb, Rossetti and Burne-Jones.

A carved glass vase with applied and *marqueterie sur verre* decoration by Emile Gallé, *circa* 1902–1904,
height 8⅝in (21.8cm)
Monte Carlo FF 516,150 (£42,728 : $68,365). 24.X.82

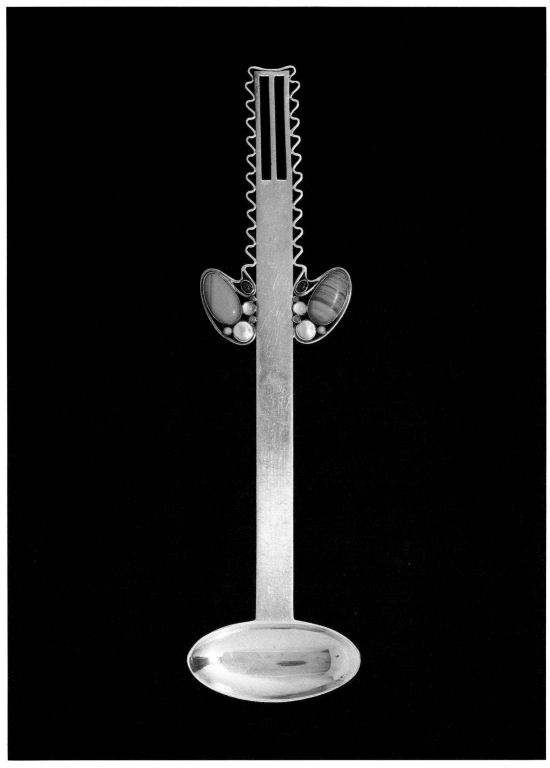

A Wiener Werkstatte spoon designed by Josef Hoffmann and made by Anton Pribil, *circa* 1905, length $6\frac{5}{8}$in (17cm)
London £17,600 ($28,160). 28.IV.83

A burr-amboyna, ivory and ebony-inlaid corner cabinet by Emile-Jacques Ruhlmann, 1916, height $50\frac{1}{4}$in (127.8cm)
Monte Carlo FF 832,500 (£68,916:$110,266). 6.III.83

A rug by Louis Marcoussis,
circa 1925,
8ft 3$\frac{1}{4}$in by 4ft 7$\frac{1}{8}$in
(252cm by 140cm)
Monte Carlo FF 167,610
(£13,875 : $22,200). 25.X.82

This rug was formerly owned
by Jacques Doucet.

A stoneware vase by Hans Coper, impressed *HC* monogram, *circa* 1960, height 23⅜ in (59.3 cm)
London £10,450 ($16,720). 29.IV.83

A Steuben glass diatretum designed and made by Frederick Carder, 1958, height 6¾ in (17.1 cm)
New York $28,600 (£17,875). 12.XI.82
From the collection of Barbara and Philip Hoover

Around the shoulder runs the motto: *STRAIGHT IS THE LINE OF DUTY. CURVED IS THE LINE OF BEAUTY.*

Jewellery

A diamond tiara, *circa* 1830
St Moritz SFr 275,000 (£82,090:$131,344). 26.II.83

Opposite
Above A pair of emerald and diamond pendent earrings
SFr 49,500 (£14,776:$23,642)
Below An emerald and diamond tiara–necklace by Cartier
SFr 286,000 (£85,373:$136,597)

The jewellery illustrated on the opposite page was sold in Geneva on 29 November 1982.

Above
A diamond brooch–pendant, last quarter eighteenth century. London £4,400 ($7,040). 14.IV.83
Below, from left to right
A diamond brooch, *circa* 1870. London £13,200 ($21,120). 14.IV.83
A diamond bracelet, *circa* 1870. London £11,550 ($18,480). 14.IV.83
A diamond pendant, *circa* 1800. London £6,380 ($10,208). 14.IV.83

Preceding page
Above, from left to right
A gold, ruby, pearl and diamond brooch—pendant, last quarter
nineteenth century. £1,100 ($1,760)
A gold, sapphire and pearl pendant by Ernesto Rinzi, *circa* 1865.
£2,200 ($3,520)
A gold *cannetille* and pink topaz brooch—pendant, *circa* 1830.
£352 ($563)
Below, from left to right
A ruby, emerald and diamond pendant, representing the cross of
the Portuguese Order of Christ. £1,650 ($2,640)
A pair of gold and enamel earrings in Etruscan *à baule* style,
last quarter nineteenth century. £1,320 ($2,112)

The jewellery illustrated on the preceding page was sold in
London on 14 April 1983.

Right
An Art Nouveau gold, enamel, pearl, opal and diamond pendant
by Vever, *circa* 1900
Geneva SFr 66,000 ($19,701 : $31,522). 13.V.83

A French Art Nouveau gold, *plique-à-jour* enamel and diamond
pendant and chain, *circa* 1900
New York $19,800 (£12,375). 6.X.82

An Art Deco gold, jade, black onyx and diamond mystery clock by Cartier, dated *1923*,
height 5$\frac{1}{2}$in (14cm)
New York $37,400 (£23,375). 20.IV.83

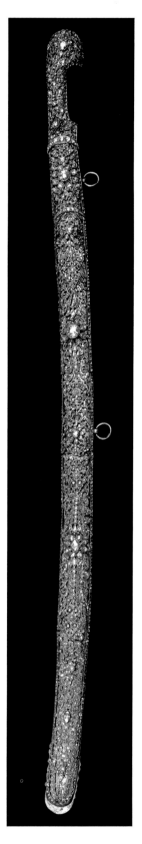

Above
A diamond necklace set at the centre with fancy blue, yellow and pink diamonds
Geneva SFr 440,000 (£131,343:$210,149). 13.V.83
Below, from left to right
A round fancy pink diamond
Geneva SFr 99,000 (£29,552:$47,283). 13.V.83
A diamond brooch, with two fancy yellow stones
Geneva SFr 88,000 (£26,269:$42,030). 13.V.83

Left
A cushion-shaped diamond weighing 74.65 carats
SFr 462,000 (£137,910:$220,656)

Right
An Imperial dress sword, the front of the hilt and
scabbard set with diamonds
SFr 143,000 (£42,687:$68,299)

This sword and diamond, formerly belonging to
Ahmed Shah Qajar of Persia (1909–25), were sold
in Geneva on 13 May 1983.

From left to right
A pear-shaped diamond (10.14 carats) pendant by
Van Cleef & Arpels
New York $308,000 (£192,500). 9.XII.82
A pear-shaped fancy blue diamond (4.13 carats)
New York $214,500 (£134,063). 20.X.82

From left to right
A step-cut diamond (26.45 carats) ring
New York $418,000 (£261,250). 20.IV.83
A pear-shaped diamond (11.24 carats) ring by Winston
New York $286,000 (£178,750). 20.X.82
From the collection of the late Helen W. Fraser

A ruby and diamond brooch, *circa* 1905
London £18,700 ($29,920). 14.IV.83

From left to right
A marquise-shaped diamond (10.04 carats) ring by
Van Cleef & Arpels
New York $308,000 (£192,500). 9.XII.82
A round diamond (19.34 carats) ring
New York $396,000 (£247,500). 9.XII.82

From left to right
A step-cut emerald (14.24 carats) ring by Cartier
New York $583,000 (£364,375). 20.IV.83
From the collection of the late Gladys Letts Pollock
An oval-shaped ruby (2.65 carats) and diamond ring
New York $82,500 (£51,563). 9.XII.82

A sapphire and diamond clip by Van Cleef & Arpels
New York $68,750(£42,969). 20.IV.83

A sapphire and diamond bracelet and clip by Cartier, 1937
New York $638,000 (£398,750). 20.IV.83

Antiquities
and Asian art

An Egyptian limestone relief, late Fifth–early Sixth Dynasty, *circa* 2300–2250 BC, height 51⅜in (130.5cm)
New York $49,500 (£30,938). 10.VI.83

The subject of this relief is identified as Ny-Ka-Teti, Overseer of One Side of the Boat of the Palace Physicians and Scribe of the Magicians.

An Egyptian granite statue of Merneptah, Royal Scribe and Charioteer, reign of Rameses II
(1290–1224 BC), height of figure 31 in (78.7 cm)
New York $341,000 (£213,125). 10.VI.83
From the collection of Chautauqua Institution, New York

This statue, which was discovered by Sir W. M. Flinders Petrie in 1887, guarded the great temple of
the Goddess Wadjet at Nebesheh and was dedicated by Merneptah's son, the Prophet Imenu.

An Egyptian chalcedony head of a horse, *circa* first century AD, length 2⅜in (6cm)
New York $18,700 (£11,688). 10.VI.83

Originally, this was probably the handle of a knife.

A Celtic bronze harness mount, first half first century AD, width 3½in (8.9cm)
London £59,400 ($95,040). 11.VII.83
From the collection of Derek Robinson

This is one of two harness mounts found in 1978 near Hambledon, Buckinghamshire.

A Neo-Sumerian copper foundation figure, probably of King Warad-Sin of Larsa,
Isin-Larsa period, *circa* 1900–1700 BC, height 10¾in (27.3cm)
New York $66,000 (£41,250). 10.VI.83

An Attic black-figure hydria belonging to the Leagros group, last quarter
sixth century BC, height 17⅝in (44.7cm)
London £52,800 ($84,480). 11.VII.83

Opposite
A sandcore glass alabastron, fourth century BC, height 8¾in (22.2cm)
London £34,100 ($54,560). 13.XII.82

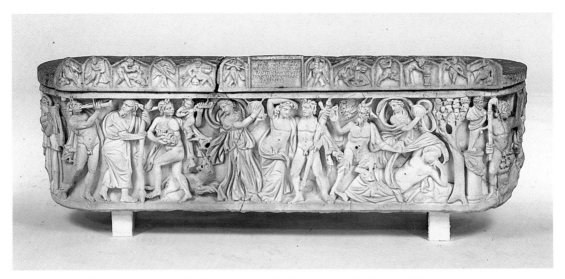

A Roman marble sarcophagus and lid for a young girl, decorated with Bacchanalian scenes, 210–20 AD, length 67½in (171.5cm)
London £46,200 ($73,920). 11.VII.83
From the collection of the Lord Astor of Hever

A Roman porphyry bath support, *circa* second century AD, length 48in (122cm)
London £34,100 ($54,560). 11.VII.83
From the collection of the Lord Astor of Hever

The Roman sculpture on this page was part of a collection formed by William Waldorf Astor, largely assembled while he was American Minister in Rome. He later placed it in the elaborate Italian Gardens which he had laid out at Hever Castle.

A Roman marble bust of the Empress Sabina, *circa* 120 AD, height 28¾in (72.1cm)
New York $154,000 (£96,250). 10.VI.83

A Kashmir bronze figure of Vajrapani,
circa ninth–tenth century, height 11in (28cm)
London £20,900 ($33,440). 29.XI.82

A Tibetan bronze figure of the Mahasiddha
Bir-Wa-Pa, *circa* sixteenth century,
height 15½in (39.4cm)
London £6,820 ($10,912). 4.VII.83

An Ayudhyā gold, ruby and pearl crown, Thailand, fifteenth century, height $7\frac{1}{2}$in (19cm)
New York $18,700 (£11,688). 30.XI.82
From the collection of Jay C. Leff

Tribal art

A Blackfoot buffalo-hide shield with two painted buckskin covers, diameter 19¾in (50.2cm)
New York $68,750(£42,969). 23.X.82
From the collection of the Tennessee Historical Society, Nashville

Captain Thomas A. Clairborne acquired this shield from a Blackfoot chief in about 1846. The bird
and snakes on the two covers are the chief's insignia, chosen in response to visions experienced
after a period of ritual starvation.

A Veracruz terracotta figure of Xipe Totec,
Early Classic period, *circa* 250–550 AD,
height 41⅛in (104.5cm)
New York $71,500 (£44,688). 12.V.83
From the collection of Jay C. Leff

A Mayan terracotta figure of a dignitary, Jaina,
Late Classic period, *circa* 550–950 AD,
height 11¼in (28.5cm)
New York $34,100 (£21,313). 12.V.83
From the collection of Jay C. Leff

The Prince Sadruddin Aga Khan Collection of African art

Roberto Fainello

The Prince Sadruddin Aga Khan's collection of African art was the first major collection to be sold since those of George Ortiz and Renée Rasmussen were dispersed in the late 1970s. He began collecting in the early 1960s as a result of his frequent missions to Africa on behalf of the United Nations, and over the following decade and a half he assembled an outstanding group of objects. It was the demands of his other passion, Islamic art, that prompted him to auction them last June.

Many major cultural areas in Africa were represented, and there were rare pieces from areas less well known from surviving material: a Hehe throne from Tanzania is one of the few objects that can be associated with this part of eastern Africa (Fig. 6). The stylistic range of the pieces is evident when one compares the abstract Songe throne (Fig. 1) with the subtle classical modelling of the Fang head (Fig. 2).

Some pieces are of special ethnographic interest, such as the Nigerian figure from the Wurbo group of Jukun-speaking peoples (Fig. 3). Dr Arnold Rubin has associated this figure with the Mam human fertility cult.

Royal authority in Africa was well illustrated by three very different thrones: the beaded Baham throne from Cameroon, the Hehe throne from Tanzania and the Songe throne from south-eastern Zaïre. Another important royal object is the Yombe chief's ivory staff finial, incorporating a figure that is probably a portrait of the ruler (Fig. 4). The staff or *mvwala*, like the sceptre, was a symbol of authority, sometimes carried by a messenger to confirm the chief's mandate.

Prominent among the pioneering connoisseurs of African carvings were French artists of the early twentieth century, including Picasso and Braque. They saw in them the same reduction of composition into essential forms that they were trying to achieve. Looking at the Songe stool in the Sadruddin Collection, it is easy to understand why artists like Derain, Vlaminck and Brancusi were also keen collectors.

A much earlier appreciation of African craftsmanship is indicated by the sixteenth-century ivory salt cellar from the Bulom tribe in Sierra Leone (Fig. 5). This is one of a large group of African ivories carved in European taste and collected by sixteenth and seventeenth-century European connoisseurs as a result of Portuguese trading. Among others, the Medici in Florence, the Grand Duke of Tyrol and the Kings of Denmark included such curiosities in their collections.

Although it is sad to see great collections dispersed, the sale of Prince Sadruddin's African pieces gave connoisseurs and museums the chance to acquire artefacts of a quality not often seen on the art market.

Fig. 1
A Songe wood royal stool, Zaïre, height 23⅜in (59.5cm)
London £55,000($88,000). 27.VI.83
From the collection of His Highness Prince Sadruddin Aga Khan

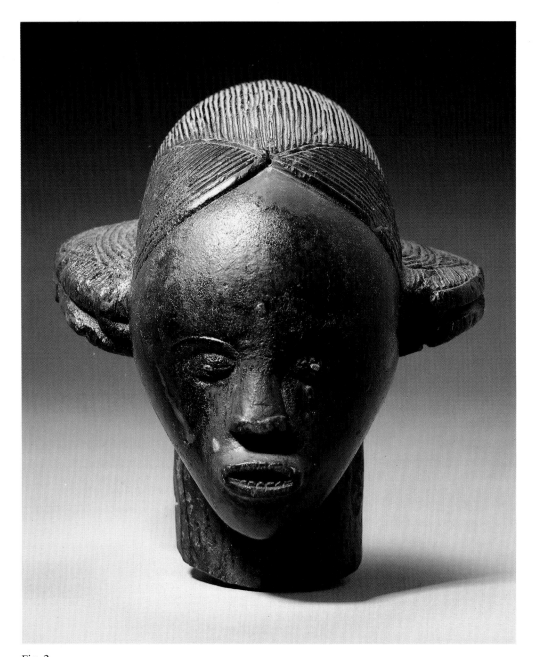

Fig. 2
A Fang wood female head, Gabon, height 9⅝in (24.5cm)
London £110,000 ($176,000). 27.VI.83
From the collection of His Highness Prince Sadruddin Aga Khan

Fig. 3
A Wurbo wood male figure, northern Nigeria,
height 32⅝ in (83cm)
London £17,600 ($28,160). 27.VI.83
From the collection of His Highness
Prince Sadruddin Aga Khan

Fig. 4
A Yombe chief's ivory staff finial, Zaïre, height 8⅜in (21.2cm)
London £38,500 ($61,600). 27.VI.83
From the collection of His Highness Prince Sadruddin Aga Khan

Fig. 5
Opposite
A Bulom–Portuguese ivory salt cellar, Sierra Leone, sixteenth century, height 7⅝in (19.5cm)
London £33,000 ($52,800). 27.VI.83
From the collection of His Highness Prince Sadruddin Aga Khan

A Hehe wood royal stool,
Tanzania,
height 31½in (80cm)
London £22,000 ($35,200).
27.VI.83
From the collection of
His Highness
Prince Sadruddin Aga Khan

Thrones of this form, carved
in one piece and with a
tripod foot, are also to be
found among the Nyamwezi
people to the west of
the Hehe.

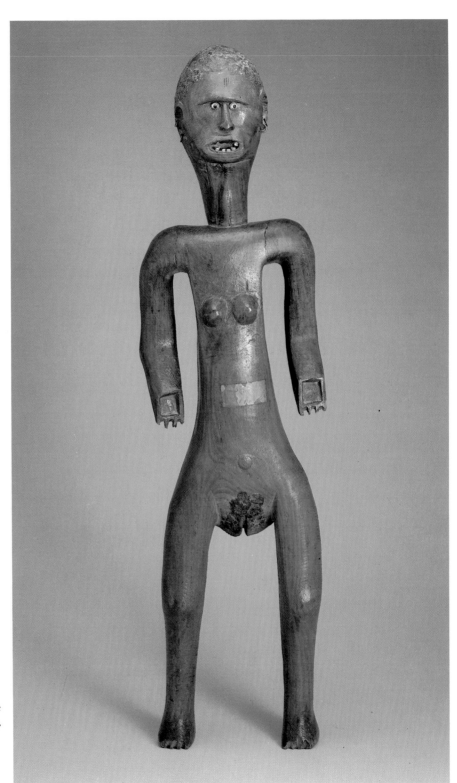

A Nyamwezi wood female
figure, western Tanzania or
eastern Zaïre,
height 29½in (75cm)
London £9,900($15,840).
30.XI.82

Figures such as these were
made as prestige items for the
court of the Nyamwezi kings,
and were also carved by
neighbouring peoples
including the Ha and
the Hehe.

Islamic textiles, works of art and ceramics

A Polonaise carpet

Donald King

It takes a thoroughly exceptional carpet to break the world-record price for a carpet at auction. This was the distinction achieved by a seventeenth-century carpet of the Polonaise type (Fig. 1), sold in a major sale of Islamic works of art last autumn.

Despite the name 'Polonaise', or Polish, which is applied, by a well-established convention, to seventeenth-century floral-patterned carpets woven with a silk pile and brocaded with gold and silver thread, these carpets were not made in Poland, but in Persia. The name, which originated in a mistaken nineteenth-century attribution, is a rather misleading one, but it has been retained as a useful label for this group of carpets and rugs, of which 250 or so have survived to the present day. Already at a somewhat earlier date, in the sixteenth century, magnificent carpets in silk, silver and gold had been woven in Persia; the finest examples are the great carpets depicting hunting scenes in the former Imperial Collection in Vienna and in the Swedish Royal Collection in Stockholm (Fig. 2). These sixteenth-century pieces are generally attributed to the city of Kashan. It is known that silk-and-gold rugs were woven in that city for King Sigismund III of Poland in 1602, and Paul Simon, a Polish Carmelite father who visited Kashan in 1608, mentions such rugs amongst its manufactures. But rugs of this kind were also woven in the *karkhanas* or state manufactories established by Shah Abbas I (1587–1628) in the new capital which he set up at Isfahan in 1597–98. John Fryer, who visited Isfahan in 1676, mentions special bazaars dealing with choice commodities such as rugs 'both woollen and silk, intermixed with Gold and Silver very costly, which are the peculiar manufacture of this country'. The Polish Jesuit, Krusinski, who was in Isfahan in the early eighteenth century, reports that the state manufactories worked not only to supply the court, but that their silk rugs and textiles were also distributed by government salesmen to Europe and to India. Although surviving Polonaise carpets of the seventeenth century are often attributed to Isfahan, there is really no reliable criterion to distinguish those made there from others which may have been made in Kashan or elsewhere in Persia.

Many of the Polonaise carpets were produced for use in palaces and great houses in Persia itself. Sir Thomas Herbert, who travelled in Persia 1627–29, describes the palace of Isfahan as having 'the ground, or floor, spread with carpets of silk and gold, without other furniture'. The French merchant Tavernier, who visited Isfahan in 1664, describes the great hall of the palace: 'In the middle of the Hall was a Vase of excellent Marble, with a Fountain throwing out Water after several manners. The Floor was spread with Gold and Silk Carpets, made on purpose for the place; and near the Vase was a low Scaffold . . . cover'd with a magnificent Carpet. Upon this Scaffold

Fig. 1
A Polonaise silk-and-gold carpet,
seventeenth century, 12ft 8in by 5ft 7in
(386cm by 170cm)
London £231,000($369,600). 12.X.82

sate the King'. In another passage Tavernier writes: 'After I had exposed my Goods upon a fair Table cover'd with a Carpet of Gold and Silver . . . the King enter'd, attended only by three Eunuchs for his Guard, and two old men, whose office it was to pull off his Shooes when he goes into any Room spread with Gold and Silk Carpets, and to put them on again when he goes forth'.

Besides their use as palace furnishings, silk-and-gold carpets made admirably impressive gifts. Among several fine examples preserved at the great religious shrine of the Imam Ali at al-Najaf in Iraq, there are two with dedicatory inscriptions knotted in the pile: 'Donated by the dog of this shrine, Abbas', that is Shah Abbas I. Examples preserved in Venice are believed to have been gifts from Shah Abbas brought by embassies in 1603 and 1622. Among examples in Copenhagen, some were brought by an embassy from Shah Safi to Duke Friedrich III of Holstein Gottorp in 1639, while another was a gift from the Dutch East India Company to Queen Sofie Amalie in 1662.

The Polonaise carpet sold in October is a fine and typical example of its class. The colours, as usual in carpets of this kind, are faded but harmonious. The background is mostly brocaded with gold and silver thread and the silk pile is in soft shades of yellow, salmon-pink, light green, light blue and dark blue. In the centre is an eight-pointed yellow medallion, which, although the principal motif in the design, is neither large nor dominant; it is no more than a slightly more important incident in a repeating pattern composed of rows of quatrefoil medallions of two alternating types. Undulating lines running diagonally between the smaller medallions form large, lozenge-shaped compartments which enclose the larger medallions; stems bearing palmettes and feathery leaves wander freely from one compartment to the next. The borders also show stems, palmettes and leaves, and there are floral guard stripes.

Although the basic elements of this design are similar to those seen in Persian carpets of the sixteenth century, the total effect is very different. In sixteenth-century carpets the chief components of the design – the central medallion, the field and the border – are clearly defined and sharply differentiated by their contrasting ornaments and colours, generally strong crimsons, blues and greens. In seventeenth-century Polonaise carpets, however, the medallions, the field and the border all have much the same ornament in very similar light tones, so that all seem blended together in a rich all-over floral pattern, in which the viewer hardly distinguishes individual motifs, but is chiefly aware of a complex rhythmic movement, a kind of wave-like ebb and flow of curvilinear forms. If we may express the difference in European terms, the sixteenth-century carpets exhibit the sharp, clear logic of Renaissance art, whereas carpets like this one share the all-embracing rhythms of Baroque art.

It is not surprising that these carpets with their elaborate patterns, the bright hues of their silk pile and the glitter of their gold and silver thread, became as indispensable furnishings for the palaces and great mansions of Baroque Europe as they were for those of Persia. They blend happily with the richest kinds of European furniture, perhaps even more satisfactorily than Savonnerie carpets, whose designs are apt to be over-assertive. Any collector who seeks to recreate a European interior in the highest style, from the period of Louis XIII to that of Louis XV, could hardly do better than to set it off with a Persian Polonaise carpet. But, judging from the auction price of the present example, this is a privilege which now, as in the seventeenth or eighteenth century, is likely to be available only to the very wealthy.

Fig. 2
A silk-and-gold carpet with
hunting scenes, possibly Kashan,
late sixteenth century, 18ft 2in by
9ft 4in (555cm by 285cm)
Reproduced courtesy of
H.M. the King of Sweden

A Kazakh rug, *circa* 1820, 8ft by 4ft 8in (244cm by 142cm)
London £23,100($36,960). 20.IV.83

A Turkman Yomut carpet, first quarter nineteenth century,
8ft 7in by 5ft 10in (262cm by 178cm)
New York $25,850(£16,156). 30.X.82

A Ghashghai rug, *circa* 1860, 8ft 8in by 4ft 9in (264cm by 145cm)
London £16,500 ($26,400). 15.VI.83

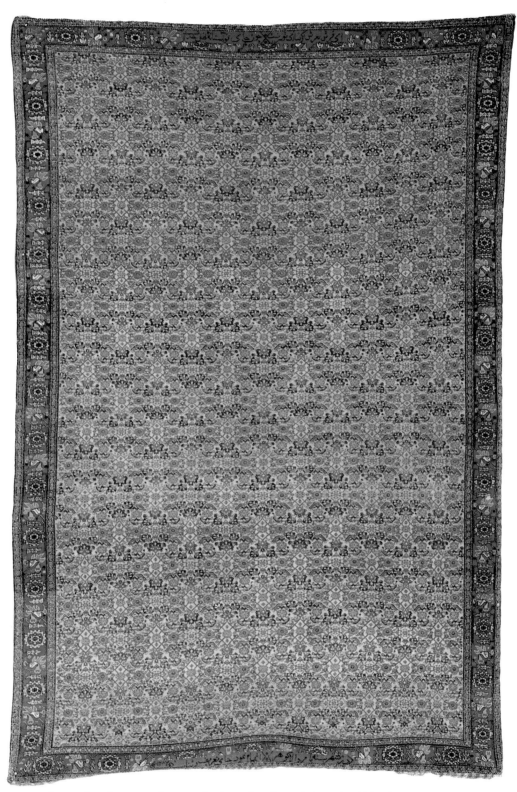

A Senneh rug, dated AH 1287 (1870 AD), 6ft 7in by 4ft 5in (201cm by 135cm)
London £39,600 ($63,360). 12.X.82

A Mamluk circular carpet, *circa* 1510, diameter 9ft 5in (287cm)
London £46,200 ($73,920). 12.X.82

This carpet, which was recently in the exhibition 'The Eastern Carpet in the Western World' at the
Hayward Gallery, London, was probably made for export to Europe as a table covering.

A Timurid silver and gold-inlaid brass jug and cover, probably Herat, second half fifteenth century,
height 7¼in (18.4cm)
London £26,400 ($42,240). 12.X.82

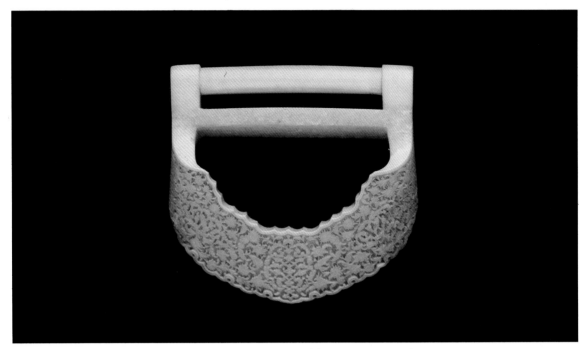

An Ottoman walrus-ivory belt buckle, second half sixteenth century, width $2\frac{1}{4}$in (5.7cm)
London £7,150 ($11,440). 20.IV.83

A Safavid open-work steel standard, late sixteenth–seventeenth century, length $26\frac{1}{4}$in (66.7cm)
London £6,050 ($9,680). 20.IV.83

An underglaze-painted pottery pitcher, Kashan or Gurgan, 1200–20, height 13in (33cm)
London £34,100 ($54,560). 12.X.82

Chinese works of art, ceramics, paintings and textiles

An archaic bronze ritual cauldron (*fangding*), eleventh–tenth century BC, height 9¼in (23.5cm)
London £143,000 ($228,800). 21.VI.83
From the collection of Madame Rollin-Austin

A Neolithic Banshan-style pottery jar, Yangshao period, height 13⅜in (34cm)
New York $42,900 (£26,813). 15.VI.83

The Luboshez Collection of Chinese ceramics and works of art

James Lally

Art collecting in China has a venerable tradition. Respect for the accomplishments of past dynasties was a fundamental tenet of the Confucian philosophy in the fifth century BC, and connoisseurship had even at that early date been long established as an essential attribute of the gentleman scholar.

During his years in China, Captain S.N. Ferris Luboshez participated in the Chinese tradition of collecting and connoisseurship in a way rarely even attempted by Westerners. An American citizen educated in London and a distinguished barrister, he served as a captain in the United States Navy and, after the war, as Central Field Commissioner for the Foreign Liquidations Commission. He had responsibility for the entire Far-Eastern theatre and was headquartered in Shanghai. Although he gained an early introduction into the select circle of Chinese collectors in Shanghai as a result of his rank and important position, it was his scholarly background and long-standing love of the arts of China that enabled him to become completely accepted by them.

As a scholar and connoisseur, Captain Luboshez seized this opportunity to develop both an understanding of Chinese connoisseurship and an 'eye' for the aesthetic of Chinese works of art. As a keen collector, he made every effort to learn the ways of acquiring the rarest and best works of art in China: he travelled widely and his friends in Shanghai gave him important introductions in Peking. The result was one of the last great collections formed in China in the traditional Chinese taste.

In a remarkably short time, from 1945 to 1949, Captain Luboshez assembled a collection of extraordinary range and quality, including archaic jades, ritual bronze vessels, pottery tomb figures, paintings and a variety of ceramics. As he became known as a collector, many pieces were offered to him privately by once-wealthy Chinese, forced by circumstances to sell treasured heirlooms, and by dealers. Other important pieces were brought to him directly from the uncontrolled excavations that were going on in the countryside throughout the period. Captain Luboshez's antiquarian taste and the unique opportunity to buy recently excavated wares combined to give his collection a bias towards archaeological artefacts, but he also acquired many fine Song and Ming Dynasty wares, as well as later porcelains.

Chinese connoisseurs have never subscribed to the Western convention that ceramics should be considered a minor art. The wealth of fine ceramics in the Luboshez Collection clearly demonstrated this. One of the best pottery vessels was a large jar with a thin natural ash glaze over a trellis pattern impressed on the exterior (Fig. 1),

Fig. 1
An ash-glazed pottery storage jar, late Warring States–Western Han Dynasty, height $11\frac{1}{2}$in (29.2cm)
New York $68,200(£42,625). 18.XI.82
From the collection of Captain S.N. Ferris Luboshez

Fig. 2
An archaic bronze wine vessel
and cover (*guang*), Shang
Dynasty, height 10½in (26.7cm)
New York $154,000 (£96,250).
18.XI.82
From the collection of
Captain S.N. Ferris Luboshez

dating from *circa* 225 BC. A simple elegance of design and complete harmony of materials and method, the essence of the art of the Chinese potter, are embodied in this piece. The beautifully modelled glazed pottery figure of a princess (Fig. 3), dating from the Tang Dynasty (618–906 AD), is another superb example of Chinese ceramic art and a masterpiece of sculpture.

Archaic bronze ritual vessels dating from the Shang Dynasty (1766–1122 BC), have long been prized by scholars and collectors; they were collected as early as the Northern Song period in the latter part of the eleventh century AD, the golden age of the literati in China. One of the rarest of these ritual vessels is the *guang*, a pouring vessel for libation ceremonies. Captain Luboshez was often told it was impossible to obtain such a piece, but his persistence was rewarded when a *guang* dug up by a farmer was brought to Shanghai by a delegation of elders from the village. After lengthy negotiations through a Chinese friend, a former mandarin, Captain Luboshez was able to buy it (Fig. 2). It was the finest of many bronzes in his collection.

Captain Luboshez has said that his greatest pleasure was the discovery, pursuit and capture of a new piece, and he took pleasure in sharing his collection with others. For these reasons he decided to sell his collection at public auction, so that others could enjoy it and continue the collecting tradition. At the landmark sale in November 1982, several pieces went to museums, but the majority sold to private collectors in Europe and America, just as Captain Luboshez had hoped they would.

Fig. 3
A *sancai* glazed pottery figure of a court lady, Tang Dynasty, height 16in (40.6cm)
New York $198,000 (£123,750). 18.XI.82
From the collection of Captain S.N. Ferris Luboshez

A glazed pottery tureen in the form of a goose, Tang Dynasty, length 14in (35.5cm)
New York $275,000 (£171,875). 15.VI.83

A *sancai* glazed pottery jar, Tang Dynasty, height 15¾in (40cm)
New York $484,000 (£302,500). 15.VI.83

A blue and white potiche (*guan*), Yuan Dynasty, diameter 13in (33cm)
Amsterdam DFl 533,600 (£117,792 : $188,467). 15.III.83

Opposite
A blue and white flask, Yuan Dynasty, height 15⅜in (39cm)
Hong Kong HK$2,310,000 (£204,425 : $327,080). 11.V.83

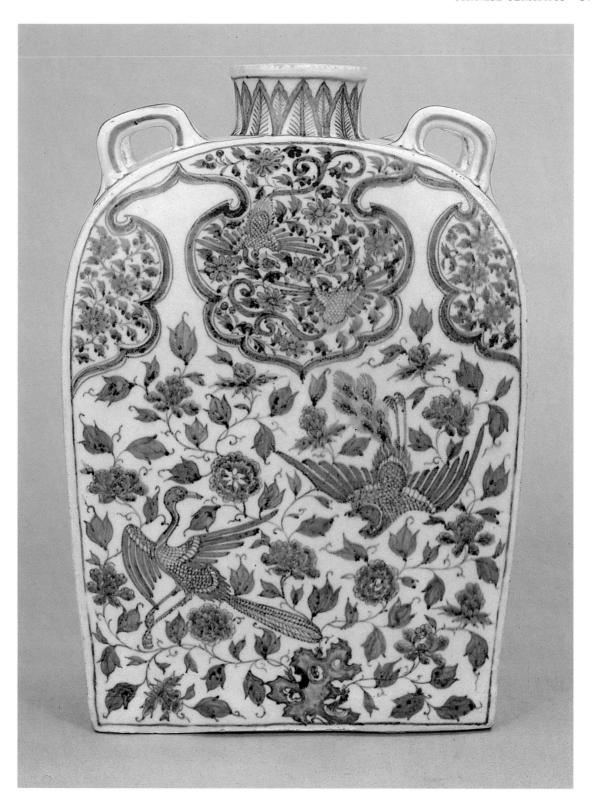

A blue and white dish, Yuan Dynasty, diameter 15¾in (40cm)
London £46,200 ($73,920). 21.VI.83

A pair of export figures of tigers, Qianlong period, height of each 22in (55.8cm)
Monte Carlo FF 333,000 (£27,566 : $44,106). 13.II.83

An ivory and lacquer snuff bottle,
six character mark of Qianlong
New York $11,000 (£6,875). 3.XI.82
From the collection of the late
Bob C. Stevens

A hornbill snuff bottle, Daoguang period
New York $20,900 (£13,063). 3.XI.82
From the collection of the late
Bob C. Stevens

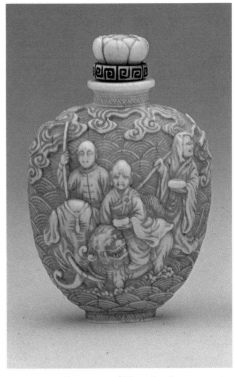

An interior-painted glass snuff bottle by
Ma Shaoxuan, signed and dated 1911
London £4,400 ($7,040). 29.III.83

An Imperial ivory snuff bottle, four
character mark and period of Qianlong
London £17,050 ($27,280). 29.III.83

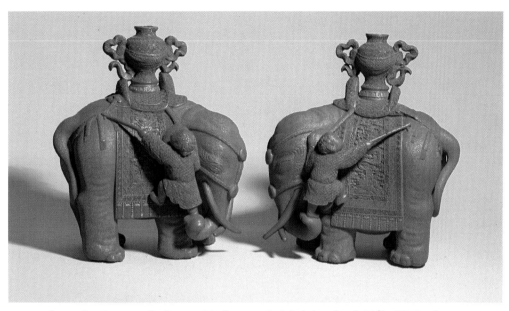

A pair of cinnabar lacquer elephants, Qianlong period, height of each 10⅛in (25.7cm)
London £16,060 ($25,696). 29.X.82

A Ming *laque burgauté* and cinnabar lacquer dish, first half sixteenth century,
diameter 15in (38cm)
Hong Kong HK$143,000 (£12,655:$20,248). 9.XI.82

A pair of Ming *cloisonné* enamel duck censers, *circa* 1600, height of each 10¾in (27.3cm)
London £46,200 ($73,920). 21.VI.83
From the collection of Frederick Knight

A pair of *cloisonné* enamel elephants, Qianlong period, height of each 15¼in (38.7cm)
Monte Carlo FF 421,800 (£34,917 · $55,867). 13.II.83

WEN ZHENGMING
Bamboo and prunus
Handscroll, ink on sutra paper, signed, with eleven seals of the artist and inscribed with a poem,
10in by 22½in (25.4cm by 57.1cm)
New York $46,750 (£29,219). 15.VI.83

Wen Zhengming (1473–1559), from Suzhou, Jiangsu province, was one of the greatest painters, calligraphers and poets of the Ming period.

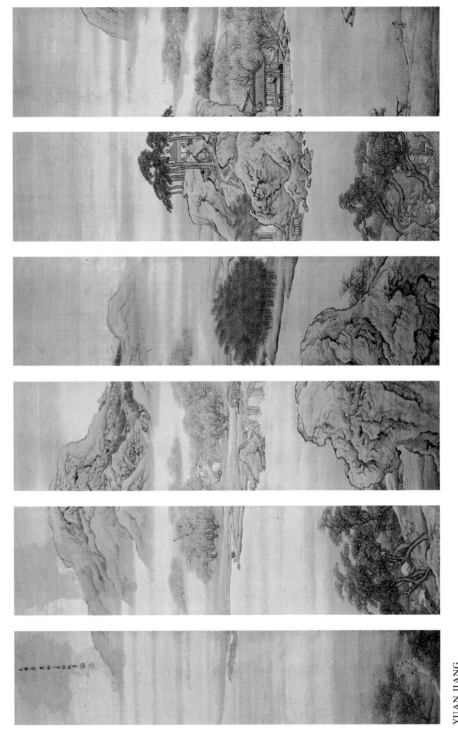

YUAN JIANG
Peach blossom spring
Six from a set of twelve hanging scrolls, ink and colour on silk, signed, with two seals of the artist and
dated 1719, total size 88½in by 287½in (225cm by 730cm)
New York $63,250(£39,531).15.VI.83

Left
An Imperial embroidery, Qianlong period,
52in by 23½in (132.1cm by 59.7cm)
New York $34,100 (£21,313). 25.II.83

Opposite
Portrait of a Manchu nobleman
Hanging scroll, ink and colour on silk,
second half eighteenth century,
113½in by 64in (288.2cm by 162.5cm)
New York $30,800 (£19,250). 25.II.83

A label on the mount identifies the subject as
Duoluo Guojian Junwang, a title reserved for a
great-grandson of the Emperor Kangxi.

Japanese ceramics, works of art, paintings and prints

A Kakiemon dish, late seventeenth century, diameter 9¾in (24.7cm)
London £12,100 ($19,360). 8.VI.83

A Kakiemon jar with a later Meissen replacement cover, second half seventeenth century,
height 10¾in (27.3cm)
London £37,400 ($59,840). 8.VI.83

A silver-mounted Shibayama lacquer vase and cover, second half nineteenth century, height 8¼in (20.8cm)
London £6,600($10,560). 21.X.82

Above
A gold lacquer *bundai*, first half nineteenth century, length 24in (61cm). $13,200 (£8,250)
Below, from left to right
A gold lacquer *suzuribako*, first half nineteenth century, width $9\frac{3}{4}$in (24.8cm). $25,300 (£15,813)
A gold lacquer *ryoshibako*, first half nineteenth century, width $13\frac{3}{4}$in (35cm). $14,300 (£8,938)

The objects illustrated on this page comprise a writing set formerly in the collection of the Japanese Imperial household. They were sold in New York on 13 May 1983.

A pair of Imperial *cloisonné* enamel vases, inlaid mark of Namikawa Sosuke, *circa* 1890,
height 17¼in (44cm)
London £22,000 ($35,200). 8.VI.83

These vases were presented by the Emperor Meiji to Admiral of the Fleet Sir Nowell Salmon, VC, GCB,
on 19 December 1897, for the courtesy he had shown to the Imperial representative at the
Spithead Review.

From left to right
A bronze figure of a farmer by Miyao, signed, late nineteenth century, height 22½in (57cm)
London £3,300 ($5,280). 21.X.82
A bronze figure of a farmer attributed to Miyao, late nineteenth century, height 28in (71cm)
London £3,630 ($5,808). 21.X.82

Left
A lacquer needle box
by Hara Yoyusai,
signed, late nineteenth
century,
height 5in (12.6cm)
London £3,520 ($5,632).
8.VI.83

Right
A lacquer *inro* by
Ganshosai Shunsui
after a design by
Ogawa Ritsuo, signed,
early nineteenth
century,
height 3⅛in (7.9cm)
London £7,480
($11,968). 21.X.82

A *shibuichi tsuba* by Shotaken Sadakatsu, signed and
dated 1849, diameter 3½in (8.8cm)
London £1,540 ($2,464). 21.X.82

From left to right
A wood *netsuke* of a *kwagen kei*, late eighteenth–early
nineteenth century
London £3,630 ($5,808). 8.VI.83
A wood *netsuke* of a heraldic lion, eighteenth century
London £4,840 ($7,744). 8.VI.83

An ivory *netsuke* of a *shishi* by
Masatada, signed, Kyoto,
eighteenth century
London £2,860 ($4,576).
21.X.82

An ivory *netsuke* of a rat by
Kaigyokusai Masatsugu,
signed, Osaka,
nineteenth century
London £9,900 ($15,840).
16.III.83

An ivory *netsuke* of a monkey
by Okatomo, signed, Kyoto,
late eighteenth century
London £4,400 ($7,040).
16.III.83

From left to right
A gold lacquer and
Shibayama sheath *inro*
by Teiun, signed,
with *ojime* and *manju*,
nineteenth century
London £4,950 ($7,920).
8.VI.83
A gold lacquer and
Shibayama *inro* by
Teiun, signed, with
ojime and signed
netsuke by Masakazu,
nineteenth century
London £3,960 ($6,336).
8.VI.83

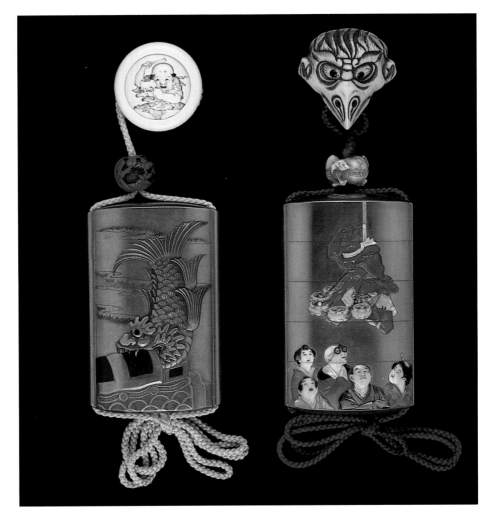

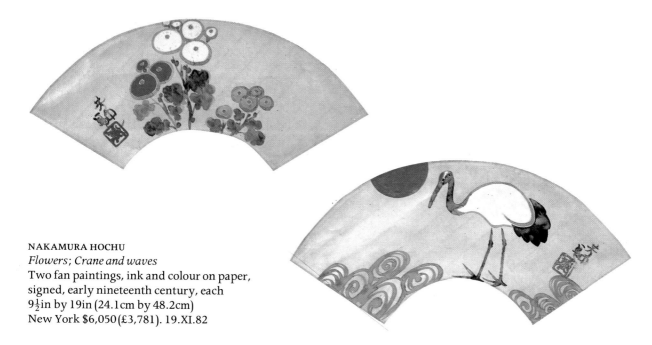

NAKAMURA HOCHU
Flowers; *Crane and waves*
Two fan paintings, ink and colour on paper,
signed, early nineteenth century, each
9½in by 19in (24.1cm by 48.2cm)
New York $6,050(£3,781). 19.XI.82

Amida Raigo with twenty-five attendants
Triptych, colour and gold on silk, Muromachi period, total size 43⅛in by 60¼in
(109.5cm by 153cm)
New York $8,800(£5,500). 13.V.83
From the collection of the late Nat V. Hammer

HOKUSAI KATSUSHIKA
Ono no Komachi
Oban, 10⅛in by 14½in (25.8cm by 36.8cm)
New York $9,350 (£5,844). 14.V.83
From the Fichter Collection

The poem illustrated in this print mourns the loss
of beauty and youth, which is likened to the
drudgery of ordinary tasks and the sweeping
away of cherry blossoms. It comes from the series
One Hundred Poems as Explained by the Nurse,
published by Eijudo and Eikodo, *circa* 1839.

HOKUSAI KATSUSHIKA
South wind and clear weather (*The Red Fuji*)
Oban, signed, *circa* 1820–30, 9⅞in by 14¾in (25.2cm by 37.5cm)
London £20,900 ($33,440). 10.XI.82

Postage stamps

MADAGASCAR, 1871 incoming cover from Oxford, addressed to a missionary's wife, bearing British stamps paying 10d to Mauritius, where a local adhesive was affixed to pay onward postage by the French Postal Service to Madagascar
London £1,100 ($1,760). 24.III.83

LEVANT, 1871 wrapper from Beirut to Manchester bearing six French 1870 Bordeaux 20c, Type I, Report I, with black anchor cancellations
London £3,410 ($5,456). 7.X.82
From the collection of Tom Roberts

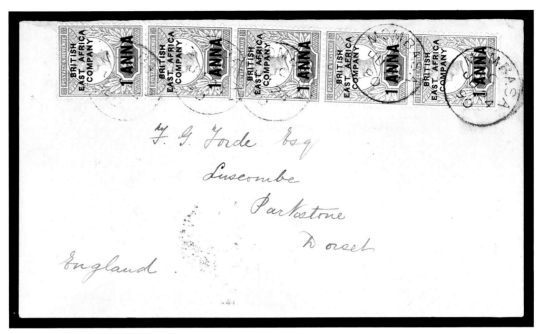

BRITISH EAST AFRICA, 1890 cover from Mombasa to England, bearing 1 anna on 2d vertical strip of five
London £5,060 ($8,096). 3.VI.83
From the collection of the late Stuart Rossiter, FRPSL

BRITISH CENTRAL AFRICA, 1891 cover from Blantyre to England, carried by the African Lakes
Corporation to Quelimane and handed over to the Portuguese authorities
London £1,595 ($2,552). 2.XII.82
From the collection of the late Gerald Simpson, FRPSL

Sir Maxwell Joseph's 'Cape of Good Hope'

John Michael

Sir Maxwell Joseph's collection of postage stamps from the Cape of Good Hope was offered on 28–29 October 1982, with estimates totalling £480,000 to £650,000. Every one of the 1,333 lots found a buyer and the auction realized £1,141,613. The sale attracted bids by post and telex from 104 people and there were ninety-five registered bidders in the saleroom, including telephone bidders from Zurich and South Africa.

The vast difference between estimate and realization is easily explained. The late Sir Maxwell Joseph was in the habit of buying collections and complete auctions intact. Thus there existed in the collection an enormous amount of duplication, together with some uneven quality. An average collection of Cape of Good Hope stamps might include six 'Woodblock' issues, a good collection perhaps thirty; this collection contained 323. In addition, there had been but three major sales of Cape of Good Hope stamps since 1967. The first, in 1970, had taken place too long ago to provide an accurate guide to today's values; the second had taken place in 1979, and the major buyers at that sale were now no longer in the market; the third sale had been held earlier in 1982, in West Germany, with good results, but with few people in attendance. So, it was decided that the collection should be offered in one sale with conservative estimates. A series of sales would create indecision in the minds of potential bidders, whereas a single sale would bring collectors to London for the auction.

The tenor of the sale was established by the first two lots. Both were letter-wrappers of the period 1652–62, addressed to Johan van Riebeeck, and in the 1970 auction had brought £155 and £105; now, estimated at £300–£400 and £200–£300, they realized £1,650 and £2,860. The demand for postal history, envelopes carried through the mails, continued unabated right through the 1851–64 triangular issues up to the 1900 'Siege of Mafeking' issues.

The 'Woodblocks' were an emergency issue, printed over a three-month period during 1861 by Saul Solomon in Cape Town. Printed on paper already full of creases, really fine examples are elusive. The letter wrapper illustrated opposite (Fig. 1) was sent from George on 23 July 1861 addressed to Cape Town, bearing a single 4d deep bright blue 'Woodblock' stamp. The wrapper had previously made £135 in 1950, and £300 in 1961; this season it realized £4,840.

The front cover of the September edition of the Cape Monthly Magazine (Fig. 2), printed by Saul Solomon & Co., folded as a wrapper and addressed to England, bearing a block of three Perkins, Bacon 1d stamps, sold for £120 in 1962; in 1982, it brought £3,190.

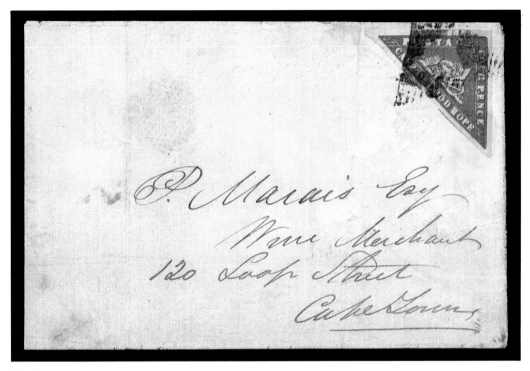

Fig. 1
CAPE OF GOOD HOPE, 1861 wrapper from George to Cape Town bearing 'Woodblock' 4d deep bright blue. London £4,840 ($7,744). 29.X.82

Fig. 2
CAPE OF GOOD HOPE, 1860 wrapper of the Cape Monthly Magazine printed by Saul Solomon & Co., addressed to England, bearing three 1d rose-red. London £3,190 ($5,104). 28.X.82

The wrappers illustrated on this page are from the collection of the late Sir Maxwell Joseph.

Collectors' sales

From left to right

A French musical automaton of a woman with a basket of flowers by Decamps, the bisque head stamped *Tete Jumeau 7*,
late nineteenth century, height 23½in (59.7cm). New York $13,200 (£8,250). 16.X.82

A French musical automaton of a jester, the bisque head impressed *Tete Jumeau 3*, *circa* 1900,
height 16in (40.6cm). New York $2,200 (£1,375). 16.X.82

A French musical automaton of a magic cupboard by Vichy, late nineteenth century,
height 33in (83.8cm). New York $23,100 (£14,438). 16.X.82

A French musical automaton of a magician by Vichy, *circa* 1885, height 23in (58.4cm). New York $6,600 (£4,125). 16.X.82

The automata illustrated on this page are from the Samuel Pryor Collection.

From left to right
A French doll by Casimir Bru, the bisque head impressed *BRU Jne 8*, *circa* 1875, height 21in (53.3cm).
London £8,800($14,080). 24.V.83
A French bisque swivel-head fashion doll in original clothes, *circa* 1865, height 19½in (49.5cm).
London £1,320($2,112). 24.V.83
A French doll by Casimir Bru, the bisque head impressed *BRU Jne 10*, *circa* 1875,
height 21½in (54.6cm). London £4,290($6,864). 24.V.83

Right
A German tinplate clockwork open tourer by
Marklin, *circa* 1909, length 9¼in (23.5cm)
London £5,720 ($9,152). 19.VII.83

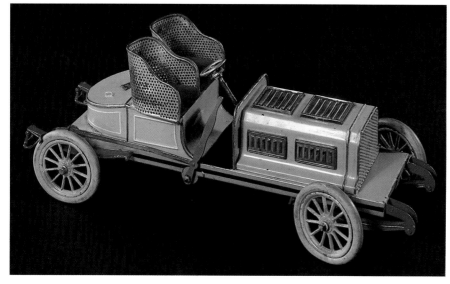

Left
A German tinplate racing car
by Bing, *circa* 1904,
length 15¼in (38.7cm)
London £4,400 ($7,040).
30.IX.82

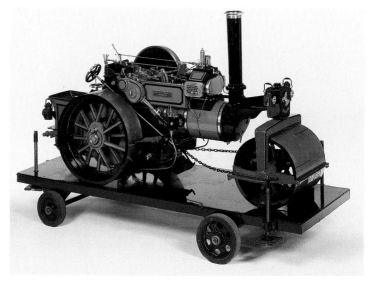

Right
An English ⅓-scale live steam coal-fired
model of an Aveling & Porter road roller,
1981, length 72in (182.9cm)
London £4,950 ($7,920). 19.VII.83

An American scrimshaw whale's tooth engraved by Frederick Myrick of the whaling ship *Susan*,
inscribed, signed and dated *Decem 28th 1828*, length $5\frac{1}{2}$in (14cm)
New York $44,000(£27,500). 25.IX.82
From the collection of Barbara Johnson

An American watercolour of a man feeding a bear a cob of maize, probably Pennsylvania,
early nineteenth century, $5\frac{5}{8}$in by $7\frac{1}{2}$in (14.2cm by 19cm)
New York $22,000(£13,750). 9.VI.83
From the collection of the late Fred Wichmann

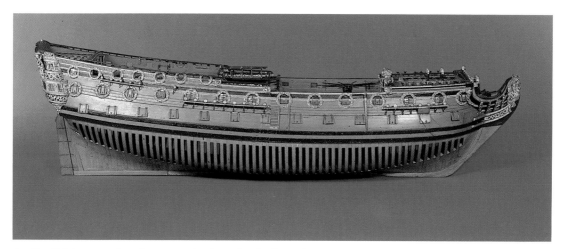

An English boxwood and pearwood Admiralty dockyard model of a sixty-eight-gun ship-of-the-line, *circa* 1700–1704, length 44in (111.8cm)
London £36,300 ($58,080). 21.VI.83

The practice of making scale models when a new warship was commissioned began during the Commonwealth (1649–53). This is possibly a model of HMS *Hampton Court*, built at Blackwall in 1701.

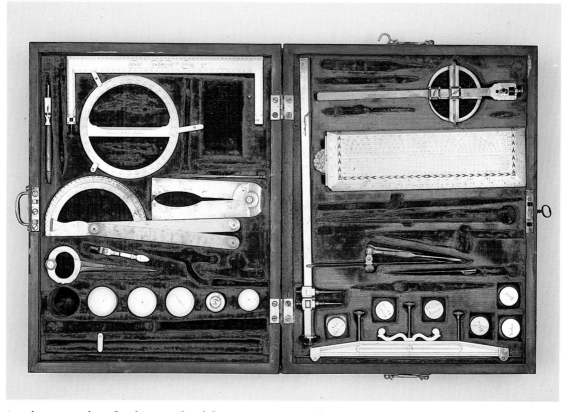

A mahogany casket of architectural and drawing instruments by Thomas Heath, London, mid-eighteenth century, width of open casket 32½in (82.5cm)
London £7,700 ($12,320). 19.X.82
From the collection of His Grace the Duke of Northumberland, KG

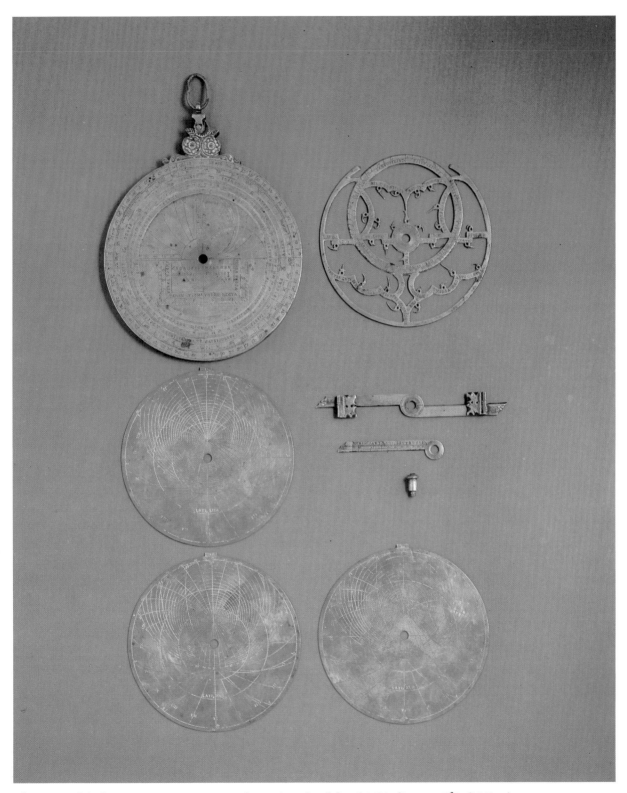

A brass astrolabe by George Hartman, Nuremberg, signed and dated 1532, diameter $5\frac{3}{8}$in (13.7cm)
New York $50,600(£31,625). 8.XII.82

Wine

Detail of a Thomason 1802 patent-type corkscrew
with a later wooden handle
London £380($608). 15.VI.83

This has been one of the most hectic and exciting seasons in the history of the department. Apart from nineteen sales in London, one each in Chester and Glasgow, and two in Geneva, which resulted in a net total of £1,853,628 ($2,965,805), the department provided the auctioneer at no less than three wine sales in California. At the ninth annual sale at Nederburg, Cape Province, the large total of R670,127 (£389,609:$623,374) was achieved.

A sale on 6 October 1982 included wines from the leading growers of Fronsac and Côtes Canon Fronsac, a lesser-known wine region but one of the oldest in the Gironde. Later the entire stock of St Olaf Bonding Co. was auctioned *in situ* on the Embankment by London Bridge.

Innovations this season have included three Saturday auctions, which have proved overwhelmingly popular, attracting many private and trade buyers who are unable to attend mid-week sales. On Bastille Day a sale of wines, mainly from the cellars of Avery's, took place at the Bristol Wine Fair. This included a magnificent range of Claret in magnums, jeroboams and imperials. Two series of outstanding wine-tasting evenings have been held at Bond Street, at which several wine growers and other experts have shared their knowledge and precious wines.

Sale prices have risen very sharply, helped by an increased demand and the strength of the American dollar. Many records have been broken and some exceptional prices have been reached. Claret remains the favourite, but a resurgence of interest has forced up the price for fine Rhône, Hock, Moselle and, above all, Vintage Port.

Right and below
A steel pocket corkscrew, early eighteenth century
London £140 ($224). 1.XII.82
A G. F. Hipkins & Son 1879 patent 'lever-rack' corkscrew
London £320 ($512). 1.XII.82

From left to right
Grand Constance 1821, the rare Constantia of the Cape, from a cellar in the south of France (one bottle)
London £380 ($608). 15.VI.83
Tokay Roos 1722, from the cellars of Augustus the Strong of Saxony, King of Poland (one bottle)
London £520 ($832). 15.VI.83
Cognac Bisquit Dubouché, Grand Fine Champagne 1811, OB (one bottle)
London £340 ($544). 30.III.83
Château Bel Air, Marquis d'Aligre, CB, probably before 1860, in a mid-nineteenth-century handblown bottle
London £210 ($336). 30.III.83
Richebourg 1964, Domaine de la Romanée Conti (one double magnum)
London £380 ($608). 30.III.83
Château Mouton Rothschild 1929, CB, one of only eight jeroboams bottled at the château
London £4,800 ($7,680). 15.VI.83

Notes on contributors

Elaine Barr is the author of *George Wickes, Royal Goldsmith 1698–1761* (1980) and has contributed articles on eighteenth-century goldsmiths to *The Burlington Magazine* and other publications. She is assisting the Department of Metalwork at the Victoria and Albert Museum, London, with preparations for the 1984 Rococo Exhibition.

Louis Cyr is Professor of Musicology and Head of the Music Department at the University of Quebec, Montreal. He lectures on twentieth-century society and music. At the moment, he is preparing a detailed introduction for the facsimile publication of the full autograph score of Stravinsky's *L'oiseau de feu*, to appear in 1985.

Laila Zamuelis Gross is Professor of English and Comparative Literature at Fairleigh Dickinson University, Teaneck, New Jersey. She is finishing a three-volume work, *Fourteenth-Century Ivories: Images in Secular Literature and Art*, and has lectured and published widely on French medieval ivories.

Michael Hodder is President of Spink & Son in the United States and was formerly the Director of Sotheby's Coin Department in New York.

Timothy Husband is Associate Curator of The Cloisters, the medieval branch of the Metropolitan Museum of Art, New York. He is a specialist in late Gothic sculpture and the decorative arts of northern Europe. His most recent publication is *The Wild Man: Medieval Myth and Symbolism* (1980), and he is preparing the *Corpus Vitrearum* volume on silver-stained roundels in the United States.

Donald King was formerly Keeper of the Department of Textiles and Dress at the Victoria and Albert Museum, London, and is President of the Textile Conservation Centre and the International Centre for the Study of Ancient Textiles. He has written and lectured extensively on the history of textiles, art, industry and trade in the Middle Ages and Renaissance. Among other exhibitions, he helped to organize 'The Eastern Carpet in the Western World', recently held at the Hayward Gallery, London.

Kenneth McConkey is Senior Lecturer in Art History at Newcastle upon Tyne Polytechnic. He has made a study of British reactions to French naturalist painting in the 1880s. His most important publications have been *A Painter's Harvest: Henry Herbert La Thangue* (1978) and the catalogue, *Sir George Clausen, RA 1852–1944* (1980). He also recently contributed a chapter entitled 'Rustic Naturalism in Britain' to *The European Realist Tradition* (1983).

Nigel Morgan is Director of the Index of Christian Art at Princeton University. He has recently published *Early Gothic Manuscripts* (1982), the fourth volume of the *Survey of Manuscripts Illuminated in the British Isles*.

Thomas E. Norton joined the staff of Parke-Bernet Galleries in 1956, and later served as a senior Vice President and Director of Sotheby Parke Bernet. Since 1980 he has been an art consultant. He is working on a book about Sotheby Parke Bernet's first century in America.

Graham Reynolds was Keeper of the Department of Prints, Drawings and Paintings at the Victoria and Albert Museum, London, from 1959 until 1974. He has written extensively on many aspects of British painting. His catalogue of the later work of John Constable is to be published by the Yale University Press in 1984.

John Rowlands is Keeper of the Department of Prints and Drawings at the British Museum. His publications include: studies on aspects of the work of Dürer (1971), Bosch (1975) and Rubens (1977); a catalogue of the prints of Urs Graf (1977); and a forthcoming book on the paintings of Hans Holbein the Younger.

Michael Edward Shapiro is Assistant Professor of Art at Duke University, Durham, North Carolina. He organized the exhibition 'Cast and Recast: The Sculpture of Frederic Remington', in 1981, and his book *Bronze Casting and American Sculpture, 1850–1900* is forthcoming. He is conducting research on marble carving and nineteenth-century American sculpture.

Lita Solis-Cohen reports on auctions and collecting for the *Philadelphia Inquirer* and is Associate Editor of the *Maine Antique Digest*. Her weekly column on collecting is distributed by the Artists' and Writers' Syndicate to newspapers in a number of other American cities. She co-authored *Americana at Auction* (1979).

Julian Thompson and John Marion are the Chairman and President of Sotheby's in London and New York respectively. C. Hugh Hildesley is a consultant to the company and the following contributors are experts: Johannes Auersperg, Roberto Fainello, John Michael and Michael R. Turner (in London); Barbara E. Deisroth and James Lally (in New York).

We would like to thank Martin Terry, Assistant Curator, Australian Drawings, Department of Australian Art, Australian National Gallery, Canberra, for contributing the note on p. 276.

A Mayan stucco head, Late Classic period, 550–950 AD, height 16¾in (42.5cm)
London £22,000 ($35,200). 30.XI.82

Index

Endpapers
MAURO GANDOLFI
Head studies
Pen and brown ink, signed *Gandolfi*, $8\frac{1}{8}$in by $11\frac{3}{8}$in
(20.8cm by 29cm)
London £1,980 ($3,168). 15.VI.83